finding LURVE
in the modern world

Helen Harman

Lothian
BOOKS

Thomas C. Lothian Pty Ltd
132 Albert Road, South Melbourne, Victoria 3205
Copyright © 2002
First published 2002

All rights reserved. No part of this publication may be reproduced, stored in a retrieval system or transmitted in any form by any means without the prior permission of the copyright owner. Enquiries should be made to the publisher.

National Library of Australia
Cataloguing-in-Publication data:

Harman, Helen.
   Finding lurve in the modern world.
   ISBN 0 7344 0428 X.
   1. Wit and humor. 2. Romance. I. Title.
A808.87

Cover and text design by Black Widow Design
Illustrations by Louise Kyriakou
Typeset by Mandy Griffin
Printed in Australia by Griffin Press

Disclaimer
The author has made every effort to ensure that the information contained in this book is complete and accurate. However, individual readers must assume responsibility for their own actions, safety and health. Neither the author nor the publisher shall be liable or responsible for any injury, loss or damage allegedly arising from any information or suggestion contained in this book.

Contents

Acknowledgements — iv

Part One — Finding Love
1. Finding ... it hard — 3
2. Finding ... the meaning of love — 12
3. Finding ... the perfect man — 24

Part Two — Finding Self
4. Finding ... body confidence — 40
5. Finding ... love with attitude — 56
6. Finding ... love with baggage — 71
7. Finding ... love with kids in tow — 95

Part Three — Finding Men
8. Finding ... love in your own backyard — 108
9. Finding ... love further afield — 120
10. Finding ... love with paid help — 151
11. Finding ... love online — 167

Conclusion
A Final Word from Aunt Lurvinya — 180

Notes — 184

Acknowledgements

This book is the result of a passionate pursuit to provide a helpful guide for anyone searching for love. It was a long time coming but it's finally arrived and I would like to extend my appreciation to all the people who supported me during the roller coaster of my writing career. I am very lucky to be surrounded by family and friends who always encourage my endeavours, even when they seem like sheer folly! I guess they knew I'd do it in the end.

For having faith in me from the start, and for his endless support, a special thank you to Carl. To Mum, what can I say? Five years of babysitting is only the tip of the iceberg. Thanks for always being there for me over the years and for sharing your wisdom, much of which permeates the pages of this book. To David, thanks for your kindness and patience, for recognising a fellow creative and for finishing the work on my study in the nick of time! To my two children, thank you for amusing yourselves for hours at a time so 'mummy could finish her book of love'. To Joan and Keira, I'm forever grateful for your help in keeping some semblance of order and peace amid the chaos. And a special thanks goes out to the family and friends who helped along the way, particularly Luisa, Liz, Janet and 'The Literary Tarts'.

An extra large thank you goes to Sharon Mullins for having faith in my original idea and being a delight to work with — and to all at Lothian for running with it!

I would also like to acknowledge everyone who shared their knowledge. In particular, Cyndi Tebbel, for going that extra mile, as well as Anne Hollonds and Fiona Papps. Thanks also to everyone whose personal experiences in their search for *lurve* helped shape the fabric of this book. You know who you are!

Last, but by no means least, I give thanks to my fabulously single sister, Chris, for her help and encouragement. This book is dedicated to you.

part 1
FINDING LOVE

1. FINDING .... it hard

Dear Aunt Lurvinya,

A few months ago, I met a man while trekking in Nepal. We ended up having an amazing holiday romance. When it came time to return home, we discovered we both lived in the same city. But he told me that he didn't want to continue the relationship. It's always the same: the guys I really like don't like me; and the ones I'm not so keen on seem ready to jump at the chance of a serious commitment. Why can't it be like it was in my mother's day? You met a nice boy, got married, settled down and had kids. Nowadays, it seems as if the good ones are either married or gay.

Miss D. Boat

Dear Miss Boat,

Ah … 'the good old days,' when a woman was expected to walk into a smoky pub, see through chat-up lines like, 'you've got nice tits', and somehow walk out arm-in-arm with her soul mate. Things seemed so straightforward then: girls with cherry-red cheeks lined the church hall and boys picked them one at a time, ripe for marriage. The truth is our mothers and grandmothers had only a small pool of suitable young men to choose from, and often settled for the best of a bad bunch. So, next time you sling your backpack over your shoulder for another adventure, think about the 'good old days' you're creating now. Would you really be happy to settle down with a local boy, or would you rather cast a wider net?

Aunt Lurvinya

The 'Good Old Days'

If someone were to eavesdrop on a group of young women in the year 2030, the conversation might sound something like this: 'Our Mums grew up during the Sixties, Seventies and Eighties, when women could achieve anything and everything. Those were the days of independence and choice: university education was free, it was safe to travel almost anywhere and women had a wide range of careers and lifestyles to choose from. They could also have sex whenever and with whomever they wanted, without committing to a long-term relationship. And, if they were careful, they could avoid the risk of an unplanned pregnancy or AIDS.'

In such liberating times, it seemed as if equality was in our sights from the day we were born. And not just for women: the men of Gary Glitter's generation even got to the chance to dance all night in make-up and high heels! However, not everything turned out quite as we expected.

Firstly, men went back to flats while our heels and hemlines continue to rise and fall with the whims of fashion. According to the style gurus, calf definition is still worth the risk of making a total twat of yourself when your stiletto becomes wedged in a tram track. And even if you happen to be one of those marvellously graceful over-achievers who can actually walk miles in sky-high heels, you're still in with a good chance of developing corns, calluses, hammer toes, fallen arches, back problems, pelvic floor strain and degenerative joint diseases. Eventually, you may even need a new knee or hip replacement! And don't be fooled into thinking the new wider heels are any better: recent studies reveal they're almost as bad. So don't throw out the stilettos just yet: they're very handy in a pub brawl or for aerating the lawn.

In their infinite wisdom, most men ditched their nine-inch heels after the 'Glitter' era. But many weren't quite so willing to give up some of the other benefits of Women's Liberation, like sexual freedom.

Isn't it 'just your luck' that when you finally meet a man who fits the bill he turns out to be a 'commitment-phobe'? He tells you he 'just wants to be friends', that he 'doesn't want a relationship *right now*', or he's just 'getting over a messy break-up'. Blah, blah, blah. You've heard it all before. The trouble is, too often you only hear it months after you've been having regular sex, or after you'd fooled yourself into thinking that you were finally onto a good thing.

According to evolutionary psychologist, David M. Buss, the caveman's desire to impregnate a woman (which could be achieved through casual sex) conflicted with her need to commit. This was because ancestral women required a serious indication of male commitment before they would consent to sex.[1] Put simply, these women wanted Dads to stick around long enough to support and protect their offspring. Has modern man achieved what the caveman could only dream of — getting his 'end away' before heading across the plains to yet another cave?

If that's the case, does it mean we must return to the days when we kept our legs firmly crossed on a hot date? Not likely. Many women also enjoy sexual freedom: from a passionate holiday romance, to the occasional cobweb-eradicating lunchtime quickie. But when it suits us, we also want a stable loving relationship. And that seems to suit us much better, and more frequently, than the type of men we're attracted to — and vice versa.

Many of us want shared intimacy, companionship, stability and the opportunity to have children within a relationship. We also want our independence and our careers. But in order to 'have it all' we need a man who's prepared to muck in. Mind you, he still has to be a 'real man'. Snags are okay, but only if they have an adequate dose of testosterone, are good in bed, have a good job, a great mind and a sense of humour. Oh, and don't forget good looks and a great bod. But a nice personality is more important. Isn't it?

TRUE TALES... *I met a bloke in the taxi queue outside a pub after closing. He seemed all right at the time, but I'd already had six glasses of Chardonnay. He asked for my phone number and, through my wine-infused fog, I relinquished it willingly. When he called, I wasn't quite sure who he was, but he sounded nice so we arranged to meet for a movie. I couldn't believe it when halfway though the film he leaned over and put his hand down my top and grabbed my boob!*

Daneka, 36

Shop Till You Drop

Many of us love the excitement of sifting through racks of factory seconds, searching for that fabulous, if slightly imperfect dress or coat. When it comes to men, however, we're reluctant to settle for second best. Unfortunately, men don't hang neatly in shops. We're forced to go out and find them.

For women with children, the hunt can be especially difficult. Past hurts, grief, loss of faith in men — not to mention the nagging feeling that there are a lot of younger, prettier, more successful women out there — only serve to make our hunt for the perfect man more complicated. With time also in short supply, we have to plan our hunt around the struggle to bring up kids, hold down a job and attempt to invent a meaningful lifestyle.

To top it off, some of us may even be emerging from a long relationship with the man we thought was the great love of our life. Instead of the relationship evolving from the bliss of the honeymoon period, it has ended in tears and recriminations. 'I gave him the best years of my life, and he gave me nothing!' Usually, once the shock wears off, your search for a new (and improved) love begins. But that search can become rather frantic, especially if you want children. So you fluctuate from believing that there really is someone out there, to thinking that all the good ones are already taken or gay. (Although statistics suggest this isn't the case.)

TABLE 1: JUST THE FACTS, MA'AM

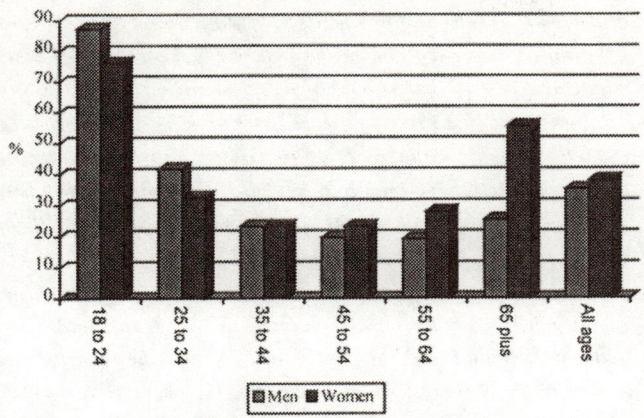

Percentage of women and men without partners (1996 ABS census)

As the table above shows, the odds of a twenty- or thirty-something woman finding a partner are still better than even. Believe it or not, there are actually *more* single men than women. For women between the ages of 35 and 44, the odds are the same. After that, they're only marginally against us. It's only in the 55-plus bracket that women outnumber men, apparently the result of life expectancy rates (their husbands start dying off).

According to projections, this trend will continue well into the 21st Century. And, if we can presume that the proportion of gay men is the same as gay women, things don't seem that bad. But let's take a closer look.

If you delve deeper into the pool, you'll discover that men are 2.2 per cent less likely to have a degree or higher qualification, and 8.9 per cent are more likely to have a substance abuse problem. When you compare single men with their partnered counterparts, the picture is grim: single men are more likely to have a lower income (or low-skill occupation), be unemployed and live in rented accommodation. Of course, these figures may confirm the adage that 'behind every man is a great woman'. Perhaps women really are the reason why married men seem more successful than their single counterparts?

TRUE TALES...

A friend from work talked me into going out with this 'really nice guy' she knew. He took me to The Pancake Parlour, ordered for me, and then spent the rest of the night talking about himself. Even when I managed to get a word in, he just carried on without making the slightest effort to listen to what I had to say.

I guess he just presumed I was enjoying his repartee, because on the way home he stopped off at his sister's house and introduced me as his girlfriend! He then told her all the wonderful things we were going to do together. I set them both straight by telling them that I was not his girlfriend and wouldn't be doing any of those things, because there was no way I was ever going out with him again. Luckily, his sister knew him better than I did and told him to stop being a dickhead and take me home. Instead, he took a detour to a mate's house. I started to panic at this stage because his mate wasn't alone: there were a bunch of blokes drinking and I was the only girl. I took a deep breath, approached the most 'decent' looking man, and told him I was scared. He told my 'date' where to get off and drove me home. In fact, he was so nice that we ended up dating for six months!

Jeanette, 27

Not Drowning, Waving

Is the pool of single, 'desirable' men actually smaller than the pool of fabulous single women? It's certainly hard to prove on paper; statisticians rarely investigate desirability ratings. Well, at least the question wasn't included in the last census. Anyway, how would they phrase it? Maybe it would look something like this:

Q.12 Are you a single heterosexual man? Yes ☐ No ☐
If yes, are you desirable? Yes ☐ No ☐

FINDING LOVE

We'd get an even more accurate picture of who's swimming laps in the menpool if they were asked:

> Are you a single heterosexual man? Yes ☐ No ☐
> If yes, place a tick in the boxes that correspond to you.
>
> - I sport a builder's crack ☐
> - I talk extensively, without interruption, on any subject, even how to breastfeed ☐
> - My superior picking skills have less to do with fruit and more to do with noses, toes and ears ☐
> - I have straggly facial hair or a broad beard with no moustache ☐
> - I always assume I am better than women at driving and reading maps ☐
> - I'm not worried about being bald because I've a great crop of hair on my back ☐
> - I wear grey vinyl zip-up shoes, loafers with tassels, thongs, ug boots, sandals with socks, white runners with jeans, or all of the above ☐

Useful? Well, at least we'd know what we're working with. I can't be the only one who thinks that an in-depth study of shoes tells women a lot about a man.

In all seriousness, once you disregard the statistics on the number of available men, things don't look that encouraging. I mean, we live in a nation where only a few years ago a Wiggle was voted *Cleo* magazine's 'Bachelor of the Year'. For those of you who haven't had the pleasure of experiencing musical hits for the under-five set, Anthony is the one wearing the blue skivvy. To give him his due, Anthony's pleasant looking, probably quite rich, obviously good with kids and his supercilious smile has an ironic edge. But, for heaven's sake, he's a Wiggle. Get a grip! If that's the best we can do on the bachelor front, then perhaps it's time to extend the theory to include: all the good ones are either married, gay, or a Wiggle. If you're over 45, add 'dead' to that list.

The Menpool

Maybe it's time to take control of the situation and improve our swimming skills before we dive into the menpool. Have you simply allowed all the good guys to sink to the bottom while you chased the impossible dreamers? If that's the case, before donning your goggles and returning to the menpool, learn how you can ditch the unrealistic expectations that may be holding you back. Important things like image, attitude problems and excess baggage. You'll also be privy to a plethora of ideas about where the good guys may be hanging (or hiding) out. Above all, it pays to keep an open mind, take an honest look at yourself, and, hopefully, by the time you've finished reading this book you'll have pinpointed exactly where you've been going wrong. Who knows, you may discover that you only *thought* you wanted love? After all, being single doesn't necessarily mean you've failed in love; for many, it's a positively liberating choice.

Tonight's The Night

Louise thinks she's on to a good thing with Phillip. He's been showering her with attention and whenever they're out with friends they only have eyes for each other. He's even nice to her children, and they adore him. Finally, someone who understands. Louise thinks that tonight could be the night. Phillip has offered to pick her up for a party, which means dropping her back home afterwards. She waxes her bikini line and slides into her best lingerie. At the party, they decide to leave early. She invites him in for coffee and he offers to take the babysitter home. Her tummy flutters as she waits for his return.

But when he does, he sits next to her on the couch, looks into her eyes and says, 'Louise, there's something I've been wanting to do for ages.'

She leans forward, lips parted.

'Your friendship is very important to me and … '

She frowns; they should be kissing by now.

' … I think it's time I introduced you to my boyfriend, Raymond.'

2. FINDING.... the meaning of love

Dear Aunt Lurvinya,

When I was a teenager, I remember waiting for love. I had a clear vision that I'd be married with children before I was 22. But when I reached that age it was the last thing on my mind; I'd just finished my teaching degree and started a new job. So, I pushed the vision out to 26. But by then, I'd developed the urge to travel and 30 seemed more realistic. Thirty came and went and, five years later, I still haven't found 'true love'. I've had plenty of romances, but the feeling never lasts. I want the kind of love you see in movies and read about in books. Is there really such a thing — and will I ever find it?

Millicent Boon

Dear Milly,

Love's out there all right — especially if you consider that each year there are 700 new Harlequin Mills and Boon titles published in Australia alone. They may be based on one gigantic myth, or maybe readers of romance novels simply like a good escape every now and then. And why not? Hollywood movies and Mills and Boon give us magical, lasting romances. Whereas, in real life, love is always a let-down — even for Tom and Nicole!

What makes you think that just because you haven't found love that life is lacklustre? Sounds like you've been doing pretty well for yourself, what with study, career and travel. Do you really think having a man make your knees tremble is better than that? Or chocolate?

Scientists have discovered that the elation we feel when we're in love is due to the release of the chemical phenylethylamine — the same chemical found in chocolate. So, my advice to you is ensure you eat plenty of good quality chockie. Then, if you happen to look up from your chalkboard and feel your heart lurch as you gaze into the 'darkly riveting eyes of a superbly muscled Adonis' — go for him! If not, does it really matter?

Aunt Lurvinya

True Love

The doorbell rings. It's Daniel. As I look into his gorgeous, deep brown eyes, my knees turn to jelly and my heart pounds. I've laid eyes on him a thousand times, but still my breath catches in my throat. With his chiselled jaw and full, sensuous lips, Daniel is truly breathtaking to behold.

'I had to see you' he says, pushing his way across the threshold, his voice thick with desire. 'I know you don't agree with the corporate takeover, but I don't see why that should spoil our friendship.'

'Friendship?' I gasp, feeling a jolt run through my entire body as he moves past me into the living room. 'We're not friends Dan, we're colleagues.'

He stops and turns. I can see the small muscles in his neck twitch; his broad shoulders seem to sag a little.

'Only colleagues?' said Dan, the ache in his voice sending a shock wave to the very core of my being.

I shake my head and mumble something about not mixing business with pleasure. But in three easy strides, Daniel has narrowed the space between us and, before I can utter another word his arms are around me and his hot mouth silences my protest ...

FINDING ... the meaning of love

(*Thus ensues a three-page description of 'the kiss' — with no mention of beer breath — followed by a seven-page narration of sweaty, unadulterated, multi-orgasmic sex culminating in a declaration of undying love by both parties.*)

As the heat begins to dissipate and reality creeps back into the sex-scented room, I become aware of Daniel beside me in bed. Our arms and legs entwined, two lovers revelling in the delicious feel of skin against skin.

Suddenly, I'm jolted from my reverie by a strange sound. It begins as a ripple, then grows into a deeply resonant crescendo. Daniel has ... farted!

I barely have time to express my shock before he smiles, grabs the bed sheets and proceeds to wrap me like an Egyptian mummy.

'Dutch Oven,' he says, laughing. As I try to breathe through the hot, noxious fumes, Daniel boasts: 'Get a whiff of that one, it's a beauty!'

Some Day My Prince Will Come

Why are there so many totally unrealistic stories of love? (Even in 'True Love', above, I should have added a little awkwardness and trepidation to the multi-orgasmic sex to get close to the truth.) No wonder we have such high expectations. Hopefully, today's kids will grow into adults who are a bit savvier about love. After all, they read books that rely on smashing myths to create humour: tales like *Hanzel and Pretzel* and *The Stinky Cheese Man and Other Fairly Stupid Tales*. We only had *Sleeping Beauty* and *Snow White*; fairy tales full to the brim with handsome princes who had enough time on their hands to rescue fair maidens, and the good sense to follow the rescue with a tender kiss and the promise of happily ever after. The trouble is, these fairy stories all end at the beginning of the relationship; for all we know, Snow White needed years of therapy after being abused by her stepmother and developed an affection for short courtiers, all of which led to a messy divorce from her necrophiliac husband.

Stories depicting great romantic love have been entrenched in the Western psyche since the Middle Ages. I blame the first: *Tristan and Isolde*. As that particular myth goes: brave knight and golden-haired princess fall deeply in love but are kept apart by duty, distance and treachery before each dies tragically of a broken heart. For the past 500 years, we've been treated to the same old formula with only minor alterations. It's the same story whether you're reading Jane Austen's classic *Pride and Prejudice* or Judith Krantz's *Princess Daisy*. Which is one reason why we're so stuck on the idea of finding our own Tristan — a man who can love with such intensity that he would die for us.

But even when we manage to see through the 'happily ever after' conspiracy, and swap high-romance for something more grounding like *Introduction to Physics*, we still can't escape a multitude of films and made-for-TV movies which, despite our best wishes, seep into our consciousness and condition our responses. Take *The Sound of Music*. Beautiful young nun meets dashing widower; they marry, run away over the mountains with his kids in tow and live happily ever after. Even *The Brady Bunch* managed to weave a squeaky-clean spell of perfect love; Mike and Carol had it all, including Alice! We may know that the Bradys are pure fantasy, but we allow ourselves to daydream all the same. Perhaps not consciously, but the ideas are bubbling away in the cauldron, and each helps us formulate our idea of 'perfect love'.

TRUE TALES...

I met Steve at the top of the Empire State Building in New York. We just started talking and I thought, 'he's just gorgeous, incredible!' I don't believe in love at first sight, but this was pretty close. We clicked right from the start. He was so easy to talk to, good company, handsome and he had a great sense of humour. Steve was simply one of the nicest guys I'd ever met. Thank goodness I followed my instincts, because Steve and I spent a wonderful weekend together in New York. When I returned from overseas two months later, I moved from Melbourne to Sydney to be with him. It's now been a year since we first met, and Steve is still a total dream.

Vesna, 30

FINDING ... the meaning of love

In the real world, the search for your perfect man begins with sifting, sorting and weeding. Yet time and time again your Tristan, or your feelings for him, falls short. You say things like: 'We just don't connect', and 'I like him, but there's no magic', or 'he kisses okay, but there's no fireworks', even 'he's nice but I don't think I'd *die* for him'.

Sometimes you meet a man who triggers feelings that wake you from your slumber with an energy that positively vibrates. 'This,' you pant, 'is the *real* thing.' Can I possibly sustain this relationship? Is it more than just a long-term affair? Then, after months, maybe even years, you realise that the intensity of your feelings has faded. Perhaps you don't love him *enough*. And because reality fails to meet your ideal of love, you decide you can't be bothered salvaging what's left.

Of course, some women are willing to put up with anything and will continue to love their men passionately through thick and thin. They give their heart, their precious depth of love, only to hear their ideal man wipe the floor with it when he eventually says, 'Sorry, babe, it's not you, it's me.' As if you didn't know. After all, a real prince would never abandon his love once he'd found her; that just *doesn't* happen. Right?

Well, it may have happened to you. Because even when your faith in love and men begins to waver, you're still prepared to search, still prepared to hope, still prepared to believe that somewhere out there there's a man who can offer you perfect love. If only you knew what it was.

Love 101

Trying to define all the fuss about love isn't easy — even for the experts. The dictionary isn't much help either. The 20-volume edition of *The Oxford English Dictionary* devotes 15 columns, over five pages in its attempt to describe a simple four-letter word. Definitions range from the simple: 'to hold dear'; to more complex descriptions, which require several other dictionaries to work out the meaning. The Internet only makes matters worse. Key 'love' into a search engine and you'll receive more than 47 million pages in under one second, including everything from 'How to Love Your Dog' to 'Wet Panty Fetish'.

Which all goes to prove that defining love is fraught with confusion. After all, one woman's idea of love is another's fetish. In his book, *Anatomy of Desire*, Simon Andreae examined the efforts of 19th-century anthropologists in their attempts to make sense of love. He discovered that, although many had travelled the world in their search, none could find a common definition of love. Everyone, it seemed, had a slightly different experience and, 'as soon as anyone tried to examine it, it began to slip through the fingers; it was just too delicate to be entrapped, too subtle to succumb, too elusive to be captured by a phrase and pinned like a butterfly ... '[1]

In her book, *Love and Limerence: The Experience of being in Love*, Dorothy Tennov, a self-described 'independent scholar,' reveals her research into the phenomenon of 'falling in love'. She reached the conclusion that a new term was needed to define the differences between 'love' and 'falling in love'. She called this unique state 'limerence'.[2]

Help Me, I'm Falling

Just because we can't always agree on what constitutes 'falling' or 'being' in love doesn't mean we don't share a common understanding of the state of 'limerence'. Indeed, most of us would agree with Tennov's description of 'limerence': 'Key features include obsessive thinking about the limerent object, irrationally positive evaluation of their attributes, emotional dependency, and longing for reciprocation.'[3] According to Tennov, limerence can strike at any time, beginning with a spark so powerful and exhilarating it can produce the most intense joy known to woman (or man). Although it is a normal, non-pathological condition, it can nevertheless bring about what Tennov calls a kind of 'madness'. When that madness is impeded or unrequited, it can lead to complete misery, even suicide. Just ask Juliet.

Whether we experience love or limerence, most of us are familiar with either a strong physical attraction or even something bordering on the intensely spiritual. This emotional state can lead to a desire for a mutually exclusive relationship and commitment. It can also help us to accept another person to the degree where their faults become just as desirable as their virtues. Social psychologist Dr Julie Fitness says love is a state of illusion that, especially during a relationship's initiation stages, can make us view our potential partners through rose-coloured glasses.[4]

TRUE TALES...

My girlfriends and I used to go to The Flower in Port Melbourne every Sunday night. Once a guy named Matt sidled up and tried to chat me up over the loud music. He was rude, crude and obnoxious, and there was no physical attraction. I walked off. But he was there every Sunday and just kept on trying. The whole time I was thinking, 'get out of here, you're dreaming.' One night we tried a different pub and who should be there? Matt!

He asked me out again. Maybe it was because he was actually sober, or maybe I was weak, but I said, 'Yes.'

It was a fun night and I found out that we actually had a lot in common. We went out a couple of times, but I lost interest when Matt

> started 'playing games'. Two months later I saw him again at The Flower and he begged me to forgive him. He promised there'd be no more games. I gave him a second chance and, after a few dates, I was hooked. Matt and I now have two kids and have been married for eight years.
>
> **Lucy, 31**

Scientists can explain falling in love as a series of chemical reactions. Apparently, when we're in love we become hyper-aware. The hormone adrenaline makes our hearts pound and our bodies ready for action, the chemical phenylethylamine produces the feeling of 'floating on air,' and oxytocin is responsible for the warm, comfortable feelings when we're kissed, stroked or massaged.[5]

That may be fine for scientists, but not everyone wants to demystify love as something that, under the right conditions, could be replicated in a laboratory. And every definition in the world doesn't explain why we fall for some people and not others. Some spiritualists suggest that love and other unaccountable emotions are a result of reincarnation — a connection to the people and experiences from 'past lives'. This may explain why I took an immediate dislike to my local butcher. ('Don't you remember eating my pet dog in 1653, you axe-murderer?!')

Paul Fenton-Smith is the founder of Sydney's Academy of Psychic Sciences and author of *Finding Your Soul Mate*. He says that we share our life paths with others in order to learn spiritual lessons.[6] Apparently, true believers can recognise a soul mate from the level of intensity at the start of a relationship. Could this explain why we fall in love? Why, out of the blue, we meet someone who triggers such an intensity of emotion, such ecstasy, that we feel as if we really have found the other half of ourselves?

> Two years into my first marriage I met Jani. He was an Italian artist and there was 'fire' from the minute we met. I left my husband, and Jani and I were together for three-and-a-half years. I can only describe it as 'the agony and the ecstasy'. We could go from intense passion to complete misery in a matter of minutes. Time and again,

FINDING ... the meaning of love

my heart was broken, and I knew I couldn't live like that. I also knew I'd probably never love like that again.

A six-year relationship with David followed, but he didn't want children. Since I wasn't getting any younger, I cut my losses and left. I was still getting over David when my sister introduced me to Trevor. The next day I overheard him telling his Mum that he'd met the woman he was going to marry. I thought he meant my sister, but over the next few weeks I realised he meant me.

I was attracted to Trevor, but there certainly wasn't the intense passion I'd felt with Jani. Within three months we were engaged and a year later, we had a child. We've now been married six years and I'm level-headed enough to know that it's better to be with someone you're compatible with, rather than someone like Jani who was my soul mate.

Danielle, 43

The widespread practice of basing marriage entirely on romantic love is something particular to Western modes of thinking (although 'Western ways' seem to be permeating every corner of the globe). In many Asian cultures, for instance, the arranged marriage is still common. The practice may seem archaic for those of us who think a blind date is punishment enough, and would rather die than contemplate having someone else (especially our parents!) select our husband. But according to psychologist Robert A. Johnson, couples in arranged marriages can achieve love, but perhaps it's more akin to 'great warmth, stability and devotion' than the life-changing explosion we tend to think of as romantic love.[7]

Scientific research suggests that this type of devotion is caused by the hormone oxytocin, which triggers the 'calmer, more pleasurable state' which can foster the stable, long-term relationships that lead men and women to protect any children born of the union.[8] Romantic love, on the other hand, can apparently be bad for the genes — particularly if no one settles down long enough to ensure the future of the human race.

From Soul Mate to Stalemate

Being 'in love' can place great demands on your partner, especially if you become too dependent on them to provide and sustain those fantastic, but fleeting, feelings of ecstasy. So, what happens when they don't deliver? In the great literary romances, obstacles along the path of love inevitably lead to disillusionment. In the real world, the honeymoon stage is marked by a sense of bliss: your partner meets your every need. But once the honeymoon is over, you notice that your once-passionate lover now prefers staring at the TV rather than into your eyes. And, after sex, he stops stroking your face and declaring undying love and simply rolls over, farts and starts snoring.

Happy Anniversary, darling! I put a Smartie in this jar every time we had sex this year. From now on, we take one out each time we make love. Apparently, there are enough here to last us the rest of our married life.

FINDING ... the meaning of love

Some couples exert a lot of time and effort trying to get 'the spark' back into their relationship. This rarely works for the long term. John Gottman, a leading research scientist on marriage, says the simple truth is 'that happy marriages are based on a deep friendship.'[9] Each relationship must progress from the initial love bond to a full complement of long-term attachment. In other words, the spark is at the beginning of a relationship for a good reason: to give couples the impetus to keep working through their differences to find common ground. Once established, it's quite normal for passion to give way to contentment. Trouble is, we're bombarded by successful 'media couples' whose relationships seem nothing more than one long bonk-fest. Instead of letting disilllusionment fester, when it seems as if the thrill is gone, we're better off accepting that all relationships move through stages. So, just because your five-year relationship isn't as exciting as year one, doesn't mean it can't still be deeply satisfying. Think of it like this: you've drunk the champagne, now it's time to settle down with a nice cup of hot chocolate!

Could it be that the majority of us simply haven't learned how to do that? With cultural messages promoting self-fulfilment at the expense of everything else, it's no wonder 50 per cent of marriages end in divorce. We put all our emotional eggs in one basket, place romantic love at the heart of marriage, and then expect it to last without fading away, although we experience many changes as we go through life.[10] As Erica Jong put it when discussing her first marriage: 'We were soul mates at one period of our lives but then our souls changed.'[11]

Weighing up the Waiting

Finding lurve in the modern world can be a very tricky affair. Should you wait for all-consuming passionate love (the state of limerence that Tennov speaks of) and then hope that you can take it from euphoria to lasting joy? Or, is it possible to achieve a state of calm joy without the initial adrenaline rush? Perhaps you need to ask yourself whether you want a short-term romantic affair or an enduring relationship — and how much you're prepared to sacrifice to attain either one.

Are you seeking a relationship because you want children? If so, can you afford to put procreation on hold while you wait for the blinding state of limerence? What if you decide to wait for limerence and never find it? (Some never do.) Do you bite the bullet and settle down with the man who makes you feel warm and fuzzy, even though there's every chance you might bump into someone at the local supermarket who takes your breath away; the one you think you knew in a past life?

If you're not willing to risk that, the only sensible thing to do is to weigh up why you want to find lurve and keep an open mind. Think about *your* definition of love and whether it's working for or against you. What you want from love needs to be the driving force in your search. So get out there and take some chances, flirt with love, have a bit of fun in the dating game and see what happens. You may not fall head over heels, but you just might meet someone who fulfils some of your love needs.

3. FINDING .... the perfect man

Dear Aunt Lurvinya,

When am I gonna find the perfect man? Just when I seem to be getting close, his true colours always come through. Most men can't even manage to put the lid down on the toilet seat, never mind aim straight. Am I asking too much to expect a bloke to sustain a successful relationship? I've been cheated on, lied to, tricked, humiliated, bored senseless, stalked and left broken-hearted. I've come to the conclusion that all men are bastards.

Signed,

Hope S. Dashed

Dear Ms Dashed,

I agree it's hard to make allowances for a man who hasn't mastered basic toilet skills. However, if we want equality we can't expect them to put the seat down for us. After all, why should they have to go to the effort of lifting it up whenever they want to waggle their willy at the water closet? Something that can't be overlooked, however, is if you haven't checked the floor before sitting down and feel a little dampness seeping through your slipper socks during a quiet contemplation. Rather than nag, why not just put your arms around his neck, look into his eyes and say, 'I feel sorry for you darling. You've been pissing for 35 years and still can't get your piddle into

the toilet. Don't worry though, you're so good at other things.'
Remember: forgiveness is a virtue.

Aunt Lurvinya

That Bastard!

Are all men bastards? According to a recent survey in the men's magazine, *FHM*, there may be something to that theory, at least in Australia. Apparently, our fellas rank as the world's second biggest bastards. (Before you despair, spare a thought for your sisters in South Africa. Their chaps topped the list!) Mind you, there were only 14 countries in the survey. If you include the places where women are treated little better than livestock, our blokes might have slipped to at least fourth or fifth place. Let's be fair: the average Aussie bloke doesn't expect us to travel in the back of the ute with the blue heeler. (Well, given half a chance he might warm to the idea.) But that doesn't mean we aren't occasionally relegated to the backseat in favour of a mate. 'Let the girls sit in the back,' he says, using the twisted logic that most blokes have longer legs and girls like to chat. It has nothing to do with the fact that he thinks we're inferior. Or does it?

English men rated much higher on the *FHM* survey — at least on the surface. Most British blokes, it seems, are happy to pay for a round of drinks, open the car door, and seem genuinely interested in making conversation and listening carefully to what women have to say. But don't be fooled. As the survey suggests, they're dead shifty. Their mild manners mask what Aussie blokes are quite open about — a terminal obsession with beer. For Brits, getting to the pub and downing as much brown ale as possible before closing is always at the back of their minds.

If you take a global view, women seem to have a broader grasp of what constitutes life's worthwhile pursuits. Granted, we may enjoy a cooling lager on a hot summer day, even a large Guinness or three (for the iron content of course). But the overwhelming male obsession with beer — other refreshing alcoholic liquids, sheds and sport — is something most women can do without on a regular basis.

Men will tell you, 'it's not just about the beer, love ... it's about mateship!' Make that competition. More precisely, who can get the most beer down their neck in the shortest possible time. When men are in a relationship, their quest to down bulk beers becomes even more important. Because, even if we don't really care how much they drink, they derive great pleasure out of finding ways to bunk off and do it behind our backs.

You could always try German men; they ranked last in the *FHM* bastard stakes. It's a long way to go, but you could always try hanging around backpacker hostels or the Lufthansa counter at the airport. Trouble is, Germany is also the home of Oktoberfest: aka 'the celebration of the gigantic beer stein'. So, it's quite likely that travelling to Munich will only increase your chance of meeting more men who love beer. In fact, there's a risk that your new man, Fritz, may force you to pack up your beloved tribal artefacts or hand-stitched teddy bears to make more room for his stein collection. Or, that when he finally takes you off on a romantic weekend away, you spend the whole trip rummaging through junk shops looking for that prized stein to complete his collection. Of course, I could have it all wrong; German men might not be interested in beer at all. I'm told many have a penchant for sausages. So, beware when Fritz comes home late from work and burps. If you ask, 'Where have you been, liebling?', he's likely to admit, 'I just had to get another bratwurst down my neck before the deli shut.'

Simple Single-mindedness

Whatever their nationality, you can be sure that when it comes to men, most will be dead keen on some pursuit that you think is totally daft. And, when they're focusing on that, nothing else can worm its way into their peripheral vision. For instance, if his mind is on the Sunday football game he's not going to be thinking about mowing the lawn, especially if you've already asked him five times. If he's thinking about sex, don't worry. Most men can keep track of a porn video *and* fondle you at the same time. In fact, it's the only time men seem able to multi-task.

Maybe it goes right back to the prehistoric era, when our female ancestors had to breastfeed the baby while preventing the other kids from falling into the newly-discovered fire, pulling the tail of a sabre-toothed tiger, or poking their eye out with dad's spear. What's changed? Well, modern women still manage to breastfeed the baby while cooking dinner, cleaning the house, keeping themselves 'nice', holding an intelligent conversation and juggling a career or two.

Caveman, on the other hand, only had to concentrate on going out and catching a bit of meat for dinner. But it needed his total attention. One blink and the mammoth steaks were off and it was back to seeds and berries. Although today's menfolk can pop into the butcher on their way home from work, they still have a one-eyed focus. This means that if they happen to pass the TAB on the way to the butcher … it's back to seeds and berries again. Of course, there are times when they can turn that intense focus to something worthwhile. Like us.

What is it With Men?

In his book, *Men Are From Mars, Women Are From Venus*, John Gray has made every best-seller list by giving his take on why men and women think differently. The popularity of Gray's books is simple — he confirms what women have known for a long time! I mean, you only have to compare genitals to realise that we're worlds apart: theirs are floppin' about, swinging around, hanging out for all the world to see. Men's genitals, you could say, are very straightforward. Especially when it comes to pleasure. All we need to do is reach out and grab the thing and, whoa! They're off. Women, on the other hand, keep their genitals tucked away, leaving the best bits difficult to find without a map and almost impossible for most men to understand.

But it goes deeper than that. There's also the mystery of

menstruation for them to consider: wildly fluctuating hormones, stomachs and breasts that rise and fall with the phases of the moon, not to mention pre-, post- and present-menstrual tension. We don't need a brain scan to recognise that we're far more complicated, but it can help to know why.

According to sex therapist Dr Janet Hall, research has discovered that our neurological wiring is more complicated than what you'll find in the average man's brain.[1] Apparently, we can think and feel at the same time (well, duh!), while men tend to focus only on one or the other. Women can get in touch with their feelings more quickly (it's all in the wiring), so when we're under stress we tend to react by showing (rather than hiding) our feelings, and we cope by relating to others. Men react with actions and feel better when they're doing something, often unrelated to the stressful situation (like playing golf).

Me Tarzan, You Jane

As well as our physiological differences, men and women also communicate differently. Gray takes it even further by suggesting that we speak entirely different languages.[2] We may use the same words, but they have different meanings. The expressions may be similar, but they have different connotations or emotional emphasis. For example, when women fully express their feelings they tend to use superlatives, metaphors and generalisations. Men, generally, don't. They're plain speakers. For women, it's a case of why use two words when 200 will do. We like to talk out our thoughts, sometimes even before we know what the outcome will be. Gray says this helps us 'tap into our intuition', while men think in silence, between the spoken words. Perhaps that explains those long, loaded pauses when you impatiently tap your feet and mutter 'rude bastard' under your breath.

TRUE TALES...

I know a lot of blokes aren't good at chitchat, but at least most make an effort. Not Peter. When we met, he was the life of a drunken party. Then we went on a date and extracting conversation from him — sober, before the movie started — was like pulling teeth. It was the longest hour of my life!

After the film, he suggested we have dinner at a local pizza shop. Because we arrived in our own cars, we agreed to meet at the car park exit. When we got there my car was facing one way and his the other. When I wound down my window, he said we were going the other way, so I turned around. But he turned, too, and we ended facing in opposite directions again. I thought it was funny but he thought I was mad.

Suddenly, a big huntsman spider crawled across my windscreen. By the time, I sorted that out Peter had zoomed off and was waiting at the next set of traffic lights quite red in the face.

I should have gone home then, but I was starving so I followed him to the pizza shop. We were the only people there. By the time the pizza arrived, he was so sullen that I'd given up trying to make conversation. I cut my losses by making funny faces with my olives just to piss him off! What a shame he never phoned again.

Kristie, 26

Feeling utterly frustrated is not the only hazard of communication breakdowns. Psychologist Dr Toby Green says much can be explained by a woman's tendency to try and translate what a man says into female language.[3] We're used to meeting a girlfriend for coffee and spending an hour or three analysing one sentence he uttered the night before. We hypothesise about every possible connotation, because if we'd uttered the same thing it would have been loaded with significance.

Pulling apart what men say might be a good way to while away a few hours over coffee, but there's no use in it. It's far better to simply take the literal translation of what he says, because that's usually all there is to it. Of course, if he utters a classic like, 'I'm just not ready to commit,' Green says it's best to cut your losses and believe him. He'll prove you right, even if you've stuck around for years hoping he really meant something else. She says that a man's need to be right is paramount, so don't be surprised if he's engaged two weeks after your 10-year relationship bites the dust.[4] At least he was honest and didn't say he'd commit when it was really the furthest thing from his mind. Pity you didn't believe him.

FINDING LOVE

TRUE TALES...

When it comes to understanding women, the older I get the more confused I become! Half the time they say one thing and mean the exact opposite. I reckon they spend too much time getting advice from their girlfriends. For example, I'm not one to rush in, but I took this girl out for dinner and we had a great time. I really liked her and I did something I never normally do — I phoned the next day to say 'thanks'. What happens? She tells a mutual friend that I was too keen so she's decided she won't go out with me again! You can't win.

David, 39

The Fear Factor

Why is it that so many single men crap their daks and pack their bags at the first sign of commitment? Social psychologist, Dr Fiona Papps, says that it's not that they don't think commitment in a relationship is as important. It's just that many don't want to be a part of it.[5] Papps believes that the reason men run from commitment has a lot to do with stereotypes. For instance, if more women felt free to explore their sexuality outside a love relationship, and weren't under so much pressure to 'find a man and settle down', men might begin to relax a little.

TRUE TALES...

When women find out that I've never been married, they automatically think there's something wrong with me. If I were divorced, that'd be okay! I don't know any blokes who wouldn't seriously want to settle down with a nice girl (if they could find one) and I'm the same. Trouble is, I've watched half my mates turn into old men under the weight of mortgages and unhappy marriages. So, I'd rather wait for 'the right one'.

It's hard to figure out just who she is though. You go out on three dates with a woman and already she wants to know where the relationship is going. How would I know? Can't women just take each day as it comes, get to know each other and become friends as well as lovers before deciding if it's long-term? There's too much pressure, and to be perfectly honest, apart from feeling clucky now and then, I'm happy on my own.

John, 42

In his book, *The Transformation of Intimacy*, sociologist Anthony Giddens explains a 'pure relationship'. His definition is that it's 'a social relationship entered into for its own sake — for what can be derived by each person from a sustained association with another; and which is continued only in so far as it is thought by both parties to deliver enough satisfaction for each individual to stay within it'.[6]

That sounds suspiciously like serial monogamy, and perhaps many men would really prefer only to stick around until the fun wears off. If that's the case, maybe it would be more sensible to stop beating our heads against a brick wall and start moving in the same direction, rather than trying to find a partner for life.

For some women, the answer may lie in our body clock: you can feel it ticking and know when you're ready for a long-term commitment, especially if you want children. If you desire commitment before the man in your life does, you have to make the decision to cut your losses and look elsewhere, or put commitment on hold until he's ready. And, as you probably already know, there's no guarantee he ever will be, at least while he's with you!

Mr Far-From-Perfect

Does an inability to commit make some men bastards? Maybe, maybe not. After all, there are heaps of married louts! In *Looking for Mr Right*, Bradley Trevor Greive says our penchant for tarring all men with the same brush has more to do with our differences, with the fact that men are simply not 'as evolved' as women.[7] In other words, they're far from perfect — just like us. Some can be funny, clever and handsome, but never perfect. Even if you already know that, you might still be holding onto the belief that somewhere out there is the man who's perfect for you. When used like that, however, 'perfect' can be a dangerous word.

You may look longingly at other apparently loving twosomes, thinking they're the 'perfect couple'. But scratch the surface of any relationship and you're bound to find some level of incompatibility. Those canoodling couples in the restaurant aren't perfect; they've simply learned to live with each other's faults, which isn't always easy.

Some women can't get past the first date without pulling the poor fellow to pieces. To be fair, some behaviours and personality traits are simply unacceptable. But there's a fine line between being choosy and being overly fussy. Author Cyndi Kaplan-Freiman gives great advice when she says 'women should never allow themselves to be physically or emotionally abused, manipulated, or forced to feel guilty'.[8] Being lied to, cheated on or stalked, is simply unforgivable. And don't fool yourself into thinking he'll change once you get hold of him. If he's showing signs of abuse or manipulation in the early stages of the relationship, imagine what he'll be like later! If you have a pattern of falling for abusive men, now's the time to take the steps that will ensure you don't get burnt again. (For more on this subject, see: Chapter 6, 'Finding love ... with baggage'.)

As for other less debilitating turn-offs, maybe women need to allow for a little more tolerance. Believe it or not, men aren't old dogs. While most can't entirely alter their personalities to suit you, many can learn new tricks. For example, if you absolutely adore a bloke whose kissing prowess is second only to a Murray Cod, why not do him a favour and tell him. He might be eternally grateful for a bit of expert tuition — and you may even learn something in the bargain. Then again, he might take offence and disappear into the night; but you'd have sent him packing without a second chance anyway, right?

What Women Wanted Way Back When

Resisting the idea of the ideal man isn't easy, especially considering that some of our assumptions aren't far removed from those of our primal ancestors. According to Simon Andreae's evolutionary point of view, 'ancestral women' were on the lookout for men with a capacity to acquire status and resources in order to provide the sustenance of any relationship: food and protection.[9]

This may explain the condition that relationship counsellor Dr Rosie King calls a woman's desire to 'marry up'.[10] In other words, we want a man who's older, earns more, occupies a higher rung of the social ladder, is more intelligent, drives a better car and owns a better house. (Not asking much, is it?) But, while many of us may still crave this kind of man, most of us no longer actually *need* him. We can earn our own money, buy whatever car we want and find our own social standing. In the case of those women who are financially independent, or experts in their field, looking for someone higher up the totem pole can actually narrow the pool of available men.

That's when it's time to start asking yourself if it's really necessary to be with someone who earns more or is more successful than you. After all, you don't need a man to safeguard your financial security; you can do that yourself. Of course, two incomes are bigger than one, and if you want children or already have them, a man's capacity to provide extra spending money does becomes more attractive. Particularly if you want to stay home to look after them. (Stay-at-home-Dads may be fine in theory, but that theory can often go against a primal desire to find a man who can bring home the bacon.)

Another primal desire to reconsider in your search for lurve is the notion of exclusivity. It may have been okay when dinosaurs roamed the earth and women needed absolute dedication from a mate to ensure the future of her offspring. Today, it can seem positively old-fashioned to expect that level of dedication. Isn't that why the heroes in Mills and Boon novels are so desirable? With their penetrating eyes fixed on the heroine, nothing can drag them away. The same can be said for the sentiments aroused in a woman who watches a man smile at a baby. That may explain the popularity of Anthony from the Wiggles.

We may think exclusivity isn't too much to ask, but time and time again we set our sights on a man who's *not* looking for a relationship, who's *not* ready to commit and who's happy to fool around with several women at the same time. While at the same time, the guys who would happily pledge undying and exclusive love at the click of your fingers are rejected for being 'too nice'. We want the muscle-bound model holding the baby in the glossy poster that adorns our dunny door, not the nice bloke with puppy dog eyes and a receding hairline. Pity.

Other than the pure aesthetic pleasure that's part of the package when you're with a hunk (*sigh*), the fact that we occasionally want to get our hands on a pair of tight buns can actually be explained by primal urges. Our human ancestors were very preoccupied — even if they didn't realise it at the time — with improving the gene pool. Today, good health in a man is a preference for women the world over. For a cavewoman, a tall, athletic man with symmetrical features and blemish-free skin was more likely to be healthy and sire healthy children.[11] Such men were also less likely to drop dead at an early age, leaving the wife and kids to fend for themselves in a hostile environment. Has anything really changed?

What Women Want Now

Since we're no longer at risk of getting gored by a woolly mammoth, it stands to reason that we don't actually need a man who's able to tackle a humungous beast with a single bound. Many of us have already come to this conclusion; otherwise, there wouldn't be so many married people. (Or short, fat old blokes with cute blonde girlfriends.) Let's face it, drop-dead gorgeous blokes are few and far between, especially since most men don't have access to our little bag of beautifying make-up tricks. (And, if they do, there's a good chance they're not playing on our team.) These days, when we judge a man by his physical attributes we're relying on general standards of grooming and cleanliness. We can be very picky when it comes to turn-offs, and rightly so. However, behind every good man there's usually a closet nose-picker. The difference is that the men we should deem unacceptable partners are the ones who can't be bothered going into the closet for a bit of a dig; traffic lights are their preferred location.

Maybe its time to ease up a bit on the entire male gender

(apart from public nose-pickers)? After all, this is the modern world. We have supposedly evolved. We don't need a man to have the things our ancestors couldn't live without. Sadly, instead of becoming more forgiving, women seem to be more critical.

Gray says that women leave men when they're emotionally and romantically unfulfilled.[12] We want a man who understands our emotional needs, who talks to us, who takes equal responsibility for household tasks and childcare, respects our choice to work or stay at home, appreciates our nurturing nature and will nurture us in return. And we want it all bundled up in one reasonably attractive package, without annoying habits and flawed personality traits. Mr Perfect.

In her book, *What Do Women Want?*, Erica Jong described the perfect man for any woman as:

> the man who loves her constantly and fucks her frequently, passionately, and well; who adores and admires her; is at once reliable and exciting; an earthly Adonis and a heavenly father figure; a beautiful son, a steady daddy; a wild-eyed Bacchic lover and a calm, sober, but still funny friend. Can you find all these attributes in one man? Not bloody likely! And if you find them, will they endure for all the various passages of your life? Not bloody likely.[13]

When Less is More

Just because you may conclude that the perfect man doesn't exist, you're not necessarily settling for second-best if you refine your search to Mr Imperfect. It may just mean it's time to change the pattern of the 'type' of man you go out with. Give the decent sorts a break. Learn to live with their true colours and their annoying habits, and don't expect them to answer your question if they're concentrating on another task.

And keep fighting primal urges. Maybe you could love a guy who's shorter than you are (ask Nicole Kidman), who earns less, who needs some tuition on how to squeeze a toothpaste tube, or who's happy not being a CEO.

It's worth considering whether Mr OK really is *okay*? Because he's out there, decent but flawed. And finding him will be easier than finding Mr Everything, if not exactly cut and dried. You've still got to meet someone whose faults fall into your 'acceptable' category and who thinks your faults are 'cute'. You've got to find someone who's willing to commit to a relationship when you are, and that's often the trickiest part.

The problem is, men don't talk much about their feelings, so we never seem to know what's going on. How can we when our brains are so different? Men probably have their own version of the perfect woman, their own ideas of when to settle down. Maybe you should ask a bloke to explain it all? He could even write a book about it. You'd read it with one eye, of course; the other would be watching the spaghetti, the kids, guiding the lipstick across your lips and skimming a document for work. Multi-tasking is a beautiful thing. Aren't you glad you're a woman?

You Know He's a Bastard When...

He denies there's someone else, even when you come home early and see two imprints on the bed.

You find out that there's 'another woman' when you see her wearing the same dress he bought you for Christmas.

You start a relationship with your male housemate and go overseas together. When you return, your female flatmate hands your boyfriend her newborn baby and says, 'Meet Dad'.

You find out that the guy you've been dating is already engaged. He just needed someone to keep him occupied while his fiancée was setting up house in a city two hours away.

You arrange to spend Christmas with your long-distance lover at a friend's place. He phones your friend that morning and asks her to tell you that he's not coming, because he's decided to move back in with his wife.

He comes back from a skiing trip and calls you Dianne. Your name is Joanne.

FINDING ... the perfect man

part 2
FINDING SELF

4. FINDING .... body confidence

Dear Aunt Lurvinya,

My last boyfriend wanted to leave the lights on during sex but I didn't want him to see the cellulite on my thighs. I'm sure that's why we split up. There are just so many beautiful, thin women out there. If I don't find a way of keeping my weight down, how can I ever find and keep a man?

Di Etting

Dear Di,

I'm not going to lie to you — men love to ogle drop-dead gorgeous women. But if every man you met harboured a desire to get in your pants, how would you ever know that he really loved you, not just your looks? What's more, many gorgeous women say they never get asked out at all because they're too unapproachable!

Attracting fellas is all about whether the vibes you give off show you're happy and confident in yourself. It's got nothing to do with weight. So, throw away your scales and start concentrating on what's on the inside. Can't bear looking in the mirror? Well, shift your focus — you'll be amazed how much better you'll feel doing something good for someone else.

I'm not suggesting you give your Manolo Blahniks to St Vinnie's, but there are lots of sensible things you can do to make this crazy world a better place. From looking after the kid next door so his Mum can have an aromatherapy bath, to stepping out of your career for a year or two to volunteer abroad. Anything to stop yourself obsessing over the fact that you aren't thin, married, whatever.

Once you stop obsessing about the things you can't change, people will start to notice and admire you for the things you do. You'll make new friends, maybe even meet a man who you can make love to with all the lights on. ('Bugger the blubber, I saved a whale today!') If your fella wants the light on, it's because he wants to see you, not the skinny girls in the magazines. He can look at them anytime; they're so everywhere, they're passé. So, shed the shrinking violet act and keep the kilos, the world will be a better place for having you in it.

Aunt Lurvinya

Do You Look like Shit or Just Feel Like Shit?

We're surrounded by images of beautiful skinny women. Lean, smooth, hairless bodies, big almond eyes, pert noses, dazzling white teeth, luscious lips, long lashes, flawless skin... And don't they look fabulous? No wonder when some of us look in the mirror we think: 'If only I could lose a few kilos, if only my hips weren't so *child-bearing*, if only my stomach was flat. Why can't I control myself and stop eating so much? I'm on the zone diet. I'm using a massager on my cellulite. I'm thinking about laser treatment on my veins and facial hair. I've found this great cream for wrinkles, this wonderful new hair dye ... '

In *The Beauty Myth*, Naomi Wolf calls this obsession with our physical selves 'the secret under life that poisons our freedom'. We might have more money, power, scope and legal recognition than ever before, 'but in terms of how we feel about ourselves physically, we may actually be worse off than our unliberated grandmothers'.[1]

When we hate our bodies and become terrified of gaining weight or aging, we're doing more than just obsessing about things we can't change — we're waging war on ourselves. And do we feel any better for it? Maybe, but only until the next time we catch sight of ourselves in the mirror at a nightclub or restaurant loo. What is it with those mirrors? Are the bright lights part of a conspiracy to magnify every blocked pore and wrinkle? A few more stiff drinks may pull you through the nightmare, but the next day you rush off to the nearest shopping centre for a facial, a haircut, a new outfit and a swag of cosmetics. You get all dolled up in your new gear and return to the hunt. While bopping away on the dance floor, you begin to imagine that you're as fab as Kylie. But it only takes one visit to the loo and … wham! You're back to 'ohmigod-look-at-my-skin-my-hair-my-wrinkles-my-moustache!'

Despite decades of liberation, too many of us are too easily put back in our box by a mirror. Media analyst, Cyndi Tebbel, says there are many reasons why we feel so self-conscious:

> *So many industries are reliant on us feeling unsatisfied with the way we look. It's not so much a grand conspiracy theory, but rather that so many companies have simply cottoned on to a formula that sells products by boosting our insecurity. It works, and it makes money.*

Would we sign up for diet programs, pay thousands of dollars for cosmetic surgery, buy millions of beauty products, even some pharmaceuticals, if we were happy with the way we looked? It's probably too early to tell. But the fact remains that the fashion, beauty, slimming and media industries are based on image. Each places great value on promoting people who have one main 'talent': being photogenic. By concentrating only on the young and beautiful the media isn't doing us any favours. Because when we can't see ourselves portrayed realistically our self-respect can plummet. Time and again, the media message to women is that we are only relevant if we are young, beautiful and thin. Time to stop believing the lies.

TRUE TALES...

I was flying on the red-eye from Perth to Melbourne to meet 'the man'. So I forced myself to stay awake all night to avoid having that 'slept in' look when he picked me up from the airport.

Sally, 34

Achieving Beauty

There used to be a saying, 'If you've got it, flaunt it'. Today the message has morphed into, 'If you haven't got it, why not get it?' With cosmetic surgeons on every street corner, there's no longer any need to suffer imperfection. Just make an appointment to excise those crows' feet, trim that nose, plump up the lips and suck out all that excess fat. Germaine Greer says that it used to be a nose job here and a tit job there. Now surgeons can now remould entire bodies by shifting adipose tissue. 'Once a woman has begun surgically improving her body,' she says, 'she need never stop.'[2] Some never do.

For a great example of 'when too much is never enough', check out the fascinating website for Cindy Jackson (www.cindyjackson.com) where you'll be treated to one woman's transformation by plastic surgery. Jackson's aim is to become a living, breathing Barbie doll. In ten years she's had twenty-eight surgical procedures and is still going.

Most of us would probably agree that, after so many operations, Jackson might be taking things a bit too far. (She might disagree: since morphing into a life-sized doll, Jackson has made millions from videos and self-help books and even married her own millionaire.) We'd like to believe that beauty *is* only skin deep. It's just that we keep being reminded that it's everything. How many of us harbour a secret desire to fix that one little imperfection? Boobs, for instance.

You walk into the sailing club change room where a woman is peeling off her wetsuit to reveal a pair of full, rounded

FINDING ... body confidence

breasts with nipples that point to the ceiling. After having kids, your nipples point to the rubber shower mat. You complain to a girlfriend who tells you that the nude in question is very proud of her pert pair; in fact, her post-regatta party trick is hanging beer bottle tops from those marvellous cherries. You try this trick at home and are bitterly disappointed when the bottle tops clatter to the floor. You tell yourself *she's* the deformed one and opt for the pencil test. The rule of thumb is, if you pop a 2B under your boob and it stays there, they're on the downward turn. Well, it stays under yours all right — and you haven't even taken it out of the pencil case. In fact, as far as yardsticks go, it's pretty good, because that stayed too!

You start thinking about a boob job: average cost, $6,000 to $8,000. Even if it doesn't last (and it won't), a little lift might still be worth the pain and expense. Think of the benefits: you could prance around change rooms with pride, take part in beer top balancing competitions, go braless under strapless clothes. But only after having a general anaesthetic, being cut with a sharp scalpel and having your skin peeled back to make way for a pair of synthetic (possibly toxic) implants.

You've heard plenty of horror stories about operations gone-wrong, leading to everything from loss of nipple sensitivity to complete deformity. But those 'after' photos aren't plastered on the covers of magazines. Instead, when you open the TV guide out pop another dozen perfect pairs. And they can be yours, *if* you have the money and the nerve. Day surgery, say the ads, will even allow you to return to normal activities within 48 hours or so.

But what would your feminist buddies think? And, after all, thanks to Elle Macpherson's range of double-D bras, you still manage to hear the occasional 'nice tits' when you pass a building site. Besides, those floppy boobies can come in handy. They're the perfect place to stash your cash when roaming through foreign markets, or to pop the recipe book when you're creating a particularly tricky tidbit. (Or, perhaps that should be '*tit*bit'?) Maybe you could just get one breast done; it'd be half the price and you'd have the best of both worlds. But how would you keep a gorgeous little mound like that to yourself? You'd be pulling it out at every opportunity: 'get a look at this beauty!' There'd be nothing normal about it. You'd probably be arrested.

Besides, who was the genius who decided sagging breasts are unattractive? Men of the Azande in Eastern Sudan think pendulous elongated breasts are extremely attractive.[3] There's not much point in moving there, though. If the Azande are watching TV, they've probably already changed their minds, and prefer the prevailing silicone ideal. As Tebbel says, 'send in the clones' should be the motto of the 21st Century. 'It's never been cheaper or easier to be sliced, diced and pureed, all in the name of beauty.'[4] Ugliness has become a manufactured disease with such a high profit margin that it's now affecting men. They're joining women in the race to have face-lifts, pec implants and even penis enlargements. Where will it all end?

You're Only Worthy if You're Thin

The myth doesn't stop at beauty. Flick though a pile of magazines or surf the TV channels and it won't take long to discover that you're only worthy if you're a size ten or less. Any larger and you're a second-rate citizen.

Every now and then a new role model comes along and gives hope to those of us who haven't been a size-10 since we were 10 years old. Tebbel tried to change the status quo when she was editor of *New Woman* magazine and featured a size-16 model on the cover of the April 1997 edition. Although *New Woman*'s readership was overwhelmingly thrilled with 'The Big Issue,' Tebbel met resistance from inside the industry. When she was advised to discontinue *New Woman*'s exploration of body image, she left her job.[5]

Four years later, we saw Sara-Marie (the bouncy, size-16 star of *Big Brother*) make it onto the cover of *Cosmopolitan*'s September 2001 issue. Actually, it was the *back* cover. Flip the mag over and you'll find the size-6 Britney Spears gracing the front. I don't know how that made Sara-Marie feel, but the message to the rest of us is clear; she's not thin enough to take centre stage, her voluptuous curves must be balanced with an image of how we're supposed to look.

But how are we supposed to achieve this look unless we're genetically small framed? Stop eating? Some do. Our feminist foremothers may have fought for emancipation, but today's ideal woman is emaciated! And she's starving everywhere — in magazines and catalogues, on billboards and TV. And where are all the women size-12 and over in Hollywood? Surely, when talent was being handed out they weren't all standing behind the door holding it open for the skinny chicks?

Take Renee Zellweger. She did a great job portraying our heroine, Bridget, in the film version of *Bridget Jones's Diary*. However, if you follow celebrity gossip, you'll know that Zellweger's petite build wasn't appropriate. Before shooting began, she had to scoff a packet of donuts a day, several pizzas and pint-after-pint of Guinness to put on enough weight for the role. There's one big problem: Bridget isn't obese; she's supposed to be an average-sized woman with curves. Not only that, she looks like shit in the morning, has obsessions and hang-ups and isn't frightened of being herself. Yet, she still manages to snag (and snog) Hugh Grant *and* Colin Firth! When we read the book and watched the film we felt good. Then we saw Zellweger turn up to the film premiere in a figure-hugging, size-6 diva dress. No big pants required! That's when we realised that, when it comes to Hollywood, Bridget is just another fantasy figure.

No wonder, as Tebbel puts it, we're 'obsessed with food and worried sick about what it will do to us if we eat it'.[6] The media's portrayal of women has helped spawn an epidemic of disordered eaters and body haters.

Puberty Blues

Bad body image doesn't end if you finally manage to shed a few kilos. Even waifs get old, and these days you have to hang on to your youth as long as possible. Anyone older than 35 is simply irrelevant. I recently saw a brochure advertising sensible Italian shoes — you know, the stylish granny look? Although the shoes were definitely not aimed at the youth market, the ad featured a teenage model. What's the deal? 'Buy these shoes and you'll look like her'? Is this the image our grannies are meant to aspire to? There'll be a perfume soon: *'Pre-pubescence ... gives you the exuberant feeling of youth with subtle notes of Clearasil, strawberry lip balm, scented deodorant and an overactive pituitary gland.'*

Marketing youth as a desirable quality isn't a new concept. In fact, as Buss reminds us, the characteristics that make women attractive to men are primitive. Just as the ancestral woman chose a man capable of looking after herself and her brood, the ancestral man chose a woman with the capacity to bear children. He based this on her outward appearance of youth and health: full lips; clear, smooth skin; bright eyes; lustrous hair; and good muscle tone.[7] Sound familiar? He also kept an eye out for women with a youthful gait, an animated facial expression and a high energy level. Surely, a sign that even back then, men knew that looks weren't everything.

TRUE TALES...

I went to a Goth nightclub last year and wanted to have that wasp-waisted, busty Victorian look. Being a bit long in the tooth, I wanted to prove I could still hold my own among the pretty young things. So I wore my corset: a mighty contraption of steel and bootlaces, which I cinched as tightly as I could without breaking any bones. I had the tiniest waistline in the place, but I couldn't breathe or dance and my ribs still haven't recovered.

Krystal, 37

Reality Chick

The problem with evolution is that too many things stay the same. Men still perve on genetically beautiful young women, and those of us who don't make the grade still think we're freaks. But just because men lust after centrefolds it doesn't mean they'll fall in love with them. And here's a big note for all the women out there trying to lose that last kilo: being thin is not a signifier of youth and health. It's simply a fashion directive that has infiltrated our culture. In reality, protruding ribs and shoulder blades and pale, adolescent faces caked with make-up do not spell 'nubile'. Many models aren't even menstruating; they're either too young, or they don't eat enough! We may actually be buggering up the gene pool by going to such extremes to get 'the look'. Is that what men and women really want?

Research by psychologist Devendra Singh reveals that the amount of body fat women carry has nothing to do with the way most men rate female attractiveness. What is universally consistent is their waist to hip ratio, which apparently can be used as a measure of reproductive capability. When Singh asked men to select the image of women they found most attractive, the majority chose the one with the lowest waist to hip ratio — regardless of the cultural preference or fashion for actual body size.[8]

So, does Barbie represent the nubile, fertile young woman of our ancestral man's dream taken to the extreme? And, if so, are all men looking for her? Probably not. For one thing, Barbie's proportions are so out of whack that if she tried to walk on those tiny feet the weight of her tits would make her fall over! And if men could actually find someone with her hip-to-waist ratio (Hello, Pamela Anderson!) most would fail in their primal urge to reproduce. They'd simply be aiming too high to even get a look in.

Most of us are more likely to choose partners similar to ourselves. We may desire perfection or dream of marrying a movie star, but it's hard to meet them, let alone fall in love. Psychologist David Perrett illustrated this in studies where participants were shown a photograph of themselves which had been 'morphed' to resemble a member of the opposite gender. When faced with their replica, most people rated their own face as the most attractive face of all, *without* recognising it as their own.[9]

Of course, there are exceptions. Not long ago the media was reporting a new celebrity romance between the model, Padma Lakshmi, and the much older writer, Salman Rushdie.

Now I'm not suggesting that Rushdie is anything other than a good man with a fine mind, but do you think the teenaged Lakshmi lay awake at night gazing at the dust jacket from *The Satanic Verses* while whispering, 'Oh Salman, Salman, one day you'll be mine'? Rushdie certainly looks happy these days, and he deserves a bit of fun after the fatwa. But in her quest to partner someone of a similar calibre of beauty, Padma has failed miserably. Perhaps not in the love stakes, however. Sometimes the best matches are those where mutual attraction and similarities are teamed with enough differences to enrich both individuals. We've all heard the saying 'opposites attract', and many would agree that it's actually the differences that are exciting.

Just in case you've missed something: the way you look doesn't affect your capacity to love and be loved, unless you believe that one day Colin Firth will offer his hand in marriage. As Elle McFeast once said, 'when Cupid shoots his arrow he's aiming for your heart not your hips'.[10] Beauty certainly does not affect the quality of love you experience in a relationship. What does affect it, is how you feel about yourself. If unhappiness with the way you look is undermining your self-esteem, then it will be difficult to form healthy, happy relationships. So, what can you do about it?

Strategies for Body Confidence

1. LEARNING TO LOVE YOURSELF

How long do you spend in front of the mirror? Do you stand there sucking in your stomach, twisting around to see if your bum has another dimple, slapping the wobbly bits on your thighs, adding another wrinkle to the last count, cringing at each grey hair and bemoaning your lost youth? Well, gazing at your reflection isn't necessarily a bad thing (it's the best method to ensure sure there's no lippy on your teeth), just don't go overboard.

After all, you *are* beautiful, even if you don't resemble the women in the media. As Kaplan-Freiman says in her book *Sexy,*

Sane and Solvent, 'once we let go our obsession with having a body that corresponds to the images we see in magazines and on television, we can begin to love the body we have'.[11]

Of course, what and how we eat can definitely affect our body. But where does sensible eating end and feeling guilty about every morsel that passes your lips begin? Well, anyone obsessed with food should stay well away from fad diets. Instead, start thinking about food in terms of what you *need* to eat in order to maintain good health, rather than worry about what you shouldn't eat. Most sensible dieticians and nutritionists agree that it's far better to concentrate on developing good eating habits than to focus on 'good' or 'bad' foods. Health and lifestyle consultant Ross Smith's advice is to eat a range of foods every day, especially those that are unrefined. In addition, he suggested drinking at least 6-8 cups of fluids a day (preferably water) and avoiding too much alcohol and caffeine.[12] By teaming a sensible eating plan (never say diet) with an enjoyable exercise routine anyone can start to make the most of their good health.

As Kaplan-Freiman reminds us, 'if we feel beautiful inside, we will be more likely to look beautiful'.[13] That's why it's a good idea to start enjoying your own image and take great pleasure in whatever makes you feel good. Even Naomi Wolf says that we don't have to feel guilty about wearing lipstick. Like many feminists, she endorses glamour but only when it is 'merely a demonstration of the human capacity for being enchanted'.[14] After all, it's natural to want to be desired and to feel beautiful. It only becomes destructive if you *need* to look a certain way to satisfy someone else's idea of beauty. According to Wolf, the woman who wins is the one 'who calls herself beautiful and challenges the world to change to truly see her'.[15]

So dress the way *you* want, enjoying the visual pleasure of your reflection. Take a quick look in the mirror to check your teeth for lippy, then go out there and show the world you don't give a toss about what anyone else is thinking. Let them take what they find. It's what you do and say that will make a lasting impact, not how you look. Anyway, they're probably not even taking any notice because they're too busy worrying about themselves!

> *I realised that I was a fashion victim several years ago when my sister came over with a friend and said, 'Joanne lost a bet and she has to dress up as a tart. Can she borrow some of your clothes?'*
>
> **Chris, 38**

2. CELEBRATING DIVERSITY

What would the average person have to whinge about if we were all as tall as Amazons with legs up to our armpits, hair down to our leg pits and skin devoid of all pits? Well, the unthinkable might happen: beauty, as we know it, would become *average*. The world would become so dull we'd have to find a different set of 'unattainables' to aspire to. Maybe we'd even start wishing we were shorter, fatter, pimply or bald! Isn't it a better idea to focus on what makes us unique? As the French say, *Vive la difference*!

Look around any gym and you're sure to find lots of women in peak physical condition. A few might even conform to the media's notion of 'perfect'. But most, even the instructors, will represent a range of shapes and sizes. So, what about the style police, who say that no one over a size-14 should be seen in public, let alone in lycra? Tebbel says that, 'until we begin to view the voluptuous body as something normal and accept that variation is a wonderful part of life, we continue to deny the reality of our genetic and historical evolution'.[16] People are getting bigger; you only have to pat your Mum on the head to realise that. Unfortunately, comparisons don't end there. We're constantly weighing ourselves up against others in an attempt to create the perfect template: 'I'll have her thighs, her height, her hair ... '

What a waste of time! Enjoy your body the way it is. If you want to go to the gym, or take part in any other form of exercise, great. You'll feel better, sleep better and avoid gasping for breath when you climb a flight of stairs. But do it so you have the energy to piggyback the kids or move some furniture. Do it to feel the definition of stronger muscles, to prevent osteoporosis and other debilitating diseases. Most of all do it because it's fun. Whatever you do, don't see exercise as the magic bullet that will make you resemble someone whose only value is being photogenic.

You're smarter than that, aren't you? Surely, the women you admire should include some that have achieved more than a great figure. That may be an achievement, but it doesn't cut the mustard when compared with working hard at something you love, making a difference in your community, smiling in the face of adversity, or giving without asking anything in return. Choose women that have successfully nurtured a child, planted a garden, changed a tyre, or won a business award … NOT only those who look good on celluloid.

3. IF YOU CAN'T SAY ANYTHING NICE …

The weird thing is, men don't even notice most of the things about your appearance that *you* worry so much about. Women are far more critical of themselves *and* other women. Do you seriously think that in the throes of passion men are gonna worry about (or even notice) a bit of cellulite, or that your left breast hangs one inch lower than the right, or that you missed a patch of hair on your legs in the shower that morning? As far as clothes are concerned, the majority of men just don't get the ins and outs of your carefully planned fashion ensemble. They simply see the big picture: 'she looks good'. And different men like different pictures.

Our girlfriends notice the good points: 'I like your bag', 'where'd you get that top?' And the bad: 'I hope you don't mind me telling you this, but you need a G-string with that skirt' or 'what *are* you wearing?' Maybe you have an arrangement with a few trusty advisors who can offer constructive criticism without getting their heads bitten off. But how often have you looked another woman up and down and inwardly sneered, or whispered to a friend, 'God, I wouldn't be caught dead in that!' For all you know she could have discovered a cure for cancer that very day, yet she's been judged on her dress, or her hair, or her shoes!

Then there's the old green-eyed monster. You'll know when she's arrived when you hear yourself moaning, 'I'd kill for her hair' or 'Don't you hate her, she doesn't even have to wear make-up!' Come on girls, let's band together to put an end to this epidemic of body hatred. Let's stop reading each other's appearances; we all have bad hair-dress-shoe days, some more than others. So what? Let's compliment each other and create a new, non-competitive ideal. Tell the next woman you meet that she's gorgeous. Focus on the beautiful things about her, inside and out. Whatever you do, never, never tell a friend who's recently had a baby that she looks fat. You'll either end up with two black eyes, an ex-friend — or both. You'll blame her, 'she's changed since she's had the baby'. She *has* changed and she doesn't need you to point it out!

4. TAKING ACTION

Outraged? Believe the media's misrepresentation of women is ridiculous? Why not do something useful? As Tebbel points out, 'we owe it to our friends, daughters, sisters to change [the] prevailing belief'.[17] We owe it to ourselves.

One thing we could do to end the madness is to stop buying the products that exploit unrealistic representations of women. If you want to lose weight, get advice from a health professional rather than signing up for another weight-loss scheme. Start expanding your media diet and include sources where women are three-dimensional. Don't watch films and TV shows that only feature young, thin women. I know, you're thinking, 'No more *Ally McBeal* and *Sex and the City?*' It doesn't have to be that extreme, just try to be more selective and watch what you enjoy with a grain of salt. Remember that Sarah Jessica Parker and her sex-obsessed cohorts have been cast because of their genetic endowments, and a team of full-time 'stylists' ensures they always look their best. This is not real life. It's a fiction, to be taken as entertainment only.

When you see teenage models selling products for more mature women, the majority of whom are over size-14, don't just sit there seething ... do something! Nothing will change if we all stay mute. Perhaps more of us should be writing letters and sending emails to product manufacturers and advertising agencies that overstep the mark. We could tell them that we're not going to buy that lipstick/dress/face cream/bra/car until we see realistic women gracing their catalogues, ads and billboards.

I'll never forget an ad for undies that showed a busy mum rushing to pick up her kids from school. At least I think that's what she was doing: on screen all I could see was her petite pelvis adorned in the whiter-than-white 'big pants' that supposedly support her through the day. If that model has ever been pregnant, never mind had a period, I'll happily eat this book.

Clearly, if enough of us threatened never again to buy products that are advertised using demeaning imagery, the marketers would start to get the message. After all, their aim is to make money, and if their target audience is showing signs of discontent, they might think twice before hiring another emaciated model. Send some email campaigns to your pals — before long they'll be twice around the world. It happened with the tampon scare, which didn't even have any truth in it. Imagine what could be achieved if we sent messages about *real* injustice! Greer is right when she says 'it's time to get angry again'.[18] Women deserve a visual feast, not the bland, unhealthy morsels we're currently being fed.

TRUE TALES...

I went to the hairdressers on the day of a first date with someone special. I have long blonde curls, but the hairdresser talked me into dying my hair brown. I hated it so much that I spent the afternoon in the pool in the hope that the chlorine would bleach it. There was no change, so I stuck my head in a bucket of Domestos. My hair went blonde all right, but later that night it began to fall out in clumps. Despite that, I still got the man and we've been together for seven years. (Oh, and my hair grew back, too.)

Naomi, 35

5. FINDING.... love with attitude

Dear Aunt Lurvinya,

I'm in my late thirties and I think it's time I settled down. Not just with anyone, it has to be my soul mate. Trouble is, my week's already chokka with working all day, the gym two nights a week and study. Thursdays and Mondays are TV nights and weekends are for friends and family. How am I supposed to fit looking for love into my life? Besides, I believe love should find me.

I know my soul mate is out there waiting ... I guess one day we'll just cross paths and, bang, we'll know. But what if our paths never cross? The blokes I meet are never my type, I can tell by looking. Besides, men are intimidated by me. What can I do?

Miss Conception

Dear Miss Conception,

I don't know what you're so worried about. We've all got a chance of finding Lurve ... just like we've all got a chance of winning the lottery. And lurve is a lot like the lottery; you have to be in it to win it. Now, you're definitely about to win something, but it's more likely to be an award for having the most preconceptions about love!

You've got yourself so 'worded up' that even if Mr Right knocked at your door, you'd close it in his face with a 'not today, thanks'. It's time to toss those throwaway lines and change what's really holding you back: your attitude. As long as you hang on to misconceptions you'll never find love, or discover that you're actually perfectly happy without it.

Aunt Lurvinya

Must-Squash-Attitude No. 1: 'I Haven't Got Time'

Remember when you were a kid and it seemed like ages until Christmas or your birthday and how the weeks dragged before the school holidays? Now that you're all grown up, I'll bet that time is in short supply and you find yourself thinking, 'where did the day, week, year go?' We've become so good at fast-tracking our way to success in a 24/7 world that it's no wonder so many of us don't even have time to catch our breath. When you do manage to find a few minutes, you're probably still trying to schedule in a class or two — anything to keep you on track in your quest for self-fulfilment.

You rush in the door, check the mail, the answering machine, the emails and the mobile (just to make sure you haven't missed an important message). Then it's time to throw a quick bite down your neck before flopping in front of the TV. (Sometimes switching *on* is the only switch-off time you get.)

You feel guilty about everything, especially about doing nothing. There simply isn't enough time in the day, the week, or the rest of your life to do everything you should be doing — whether you want to or not. Then you feel guilty because, by trying to be the perfect woman, you've neglected the people who mean the most to you.

With a schedule like that, how on earth can you find the time for love? Don't despair. According to Anne Hollonds, a psychologist and the CEO of Relationships Australia (NSW), an enriched life gives you a nine out of ten chance of finding love.[1] By being knee deep in your career and doing other things you really enjoy, you'll feel happy with yourself and much more attractive to members of the opposite sex.

Unfortunately, not all busy people are happy. If that sounds like you, perhaps you need to take a good look at what's occupying your time. Are some of your activities just 'noise'? Do you really need to wash the curtains on your day off? Are you obliged to spend time with a friend you actually don't really like? If you're amazingly happy with all your activities, great. But if your career network and social circle are too narrow, perhaps you need a little adjustment. Just a tweak here and there, enough to ensure that at least once a week you're somewhere mixing with members of the opposite sex, or expanding your social circle. For example, if exercise is one of the things you're cramming into an already-full schedule then why not join a mixed gym or, better still, a running club or mixed team sport? (For more ideas on how to expand your social circle, see: Chapter 9, 'Finding ... love further afield'.)

Must-Squash-Attitude No. 2: 'Love Will Find Me'

Maybe one day the doorbell *will* ring and you'll open it and find ... Pizza Man: tall, impeccably groomed and irresistible. Before you have time to wonder what happened to the pimply delivery boy, Pizza Man explains, 'As the CEO of Australia's largest fast-food retailer I thought it was time I got my hands dirty, found out what it's like on the ground.' You willingly oblige by showing him what it *is* like on the ground, in the bed and on the kitchen table. The next time he calls, Pizza Man delivers a diamond solitaire and the promise of undying love.

It *could* happen, just like you could decide to learn Spanish today and wake up tomorrow and discover you're fluent! If that's your fantasy, it's time to wake up and smell the mozzarella. Psychologist Judith Sills says that believing we can't seek out love, that it just happens to us, is a myth.[2] Relationship expert, Nita Tucker, agrees. She says you need to adopt the same attitude toward finding a relationship as you would for any other important undertaking:

> *If you want to meet members of the opposite sex, you're going to have to make a special effort to put yourself in situations where you are likely to come in contact with them.*[3]

Unfortunately this may mean changing out of your Peter Alexander pyjamas, pulling the plug on the TV set and making a bit of an effort. Just think of it as another one of your projects. Why should the search for a mate be any different to finding the perfect pair of shoes? Both require getting off your backside to shop! And shop! And shop ...

Must-Squash-Attitude No. 3: 'I Know My Type'

Don't tell me ... accountants are boring, engineers are emotionally defunct, bankers are wankers, brickies are thickies, computer programmers are nerds, and so on. If you don't like being judged, why do you do it to men? Especially when you're doing yourself a disservice by dismissing great chunks of the population. Everyone has a story to tell, an inner life, a history.

Sadly, some of our prejudices don't stop with occupations; it can get much more personal than that. Maybe you have something against people that speak with an accent, wear socks with sandals, live in the wrong neighbourhood, or drive the wrong car. Or perhaps they're too short, too tall, too young, too old, too hairy, or bald? Tucker calls these prejudices a 'no list', a strict set of unwritten rules and guidelines used to disqualify people at the encounter stage.[4] How many things on your 'no list' have anything to do with what you're really looking for in a relationship?

A good rule of thumb is to keep an open mind, especially at the first-encounter stage. After all, at first sight a bloke might seem totally 'not your type', but why not give him a go anyway (or at least have a bit of a chat). Look beyond the gold chains, designer labels and accents, and ask yourself if you're having a good time. Does this man bring out your good qualities? Does he listen to you and respect what you have to say? Do you feel good when you're with him? By focusing on your own behaviour when you're around him, instead of what he's wearing, you'll get a better indication of how well you're getting along.

The Search for the Perfect Man

Using narrow selection criteria to choose a mate is connected with our primal urge to 'marry up'. But why on earth do we want men who are older, more powerful, richer and smarter? Isn't it better to be with someone with whom you'll have at least a 50 per cent chance of winning an argument? Sure, men still earn higher wages than women on average, but do you really need his money to bring you true happiness? According to author Stephanie Dowrick:

> We are unlikely to find lasting happiness through [people or things outside ourselves ...] There will of course be rewards when we are finally driving a smart car ... But those delights are never permanent.[5]

So instead of chasing taller, smarter, richer men, why not let the perfectly decent (albeit possibly shorter, younger and poorer) blokes do the marrying up? Blokes who simply make you feel good about being yourself!

Must-Squash-Attitude No. 4: 'I'm Waiting for My Soul Mate'

We all want to find our soul mate, a man with whom we feel such a strong bond that it's almost as if we've known him all our lives. It's the stuff dreams are made of. And why shouldn't you reach out and take someone's hand, like Meg Ryan and Tom Hanks in *Sleepless in Seattle*? Hang on a minute, though ... didn't Tom's character already do that with his first wife, before he was widowed? That's right, he got a second chance at love.

Isn't it healthier, then, to think of your soul mate as the most suitable person at the time, rather than the one you haven't met but who's probably out there somewhere? Jane's story is a great example. When she was 35, she met Jack at a conference. Both were professional, single, intelligent, confident and they got on 'like a house on fire'. They had loads in common, including an extreme sexual attraction. They were soul mates. Now, backtrack fifteen years.

At 20, Jane was shy and virginal. The church youth group formed the basis of her social network, she spent a lot of time studying in the library and she never went to parties. John was also at uni, but he supplemented his studies by joining every radical society he could find. Not only that, he worked at a club, had spiky hair and a stud in one ear, inhaled the occasional spliff and made the most of the sexual freedom on campus (or anywhere else he could find it).

Chances are, that if this star-crossed pair had met at uni, they'd never have fallen in love. Had John's gaze met Jane's across a crowded cafeteria, she'd have probably blushed before looking the other way. But as Olivia Newton-John discovered when she was wooed by John Travolta in *Grease*, swapping a twinset and pearls for a pair of capri pants and a racy hairstyle led straight into the duet, 'You're the one that I want'. In real life, such transformations are much slower. And as Jane and John found out, there is a 'right time' for everyone to find their perfect match.

According to Toby Green, it's all about 'readiness'. 'When you're ready for a relationship, the person sitting next to you on the bus could be *the* one,' she says.[6] If you're still waiting, perhaps you're just not ready; or your preconceptions are holding you back. Or maybe there's a deep-seated need that requires further exploration. (For more on this topic, see: Chapter 6, 'Finding ... love with baggage'.)

Must-Squash-Attitude No. 5: 'When I Meet the Right One, I'll Know'

Did all your partnered friends know the minute they met their paramours that they'd end up together? Some did, most probably didn't. Either way, one thing is certain, at some stage in their relationship the chemistry was right. Green believes that chemistry is paramount in a relationship. 'It means magnetism, sensuality, being turned on, animal attraction. If chemistry exists, it exists, and if it doesn't, forget it,' she says.[7] That's not to say it has to happen the instant you meet someone, or that you'll live happily ever after with the man who brings on an instant hot flush. (It could just be menopause!)

TRUE TALES...

When I first met Gavin, I thought that he was the most arrogant man I'd ever met. Despite this, my friend talked me into 'doing her a favour' so I accompanied him to a ball. (Apparently she'd had a better offer since asking him and needed to palm him off.) It was a disaster. We insulted each other all night and he left early.

A year later, I saw him at a pub and decided to be polite. I said, 'hello' but he pretended not to remember my name. (I later found out that he'd actually bragged to his friends that I was the woman he would marry.) After I reminded him who I was, he bought me a drink and we talked about football.

Geelong were playing Essendon the following week and we made a bet that if Essendon beat Geelong I would cook him a gourmet meal but if Geelong beat Essendon he had to take me to dinner at a restaurant of my choice. I presumed Essendon would win, and had already decided not to honour the bet.

By some miracle, Geelong won by a goal. Not only did he honour the bet but he took me to the most expensive restaurant in town. To my amazement, we had a fantastic evening. He rang me the next day and asked me to the movies. For the next two weeks, we saw each other every day, then he moved into my house. We were married two years later.

Kaye, 33

You've probably heard loads of stories about how love can grow or creep up on you, and of long-term friends who suddenly become lovers. In such cases, chemistry happens a bit further down the track, as a result of the admiration and respect that only develops after you really get to know someone. That is a much better basis for a deeply passionate, committed relationship because you fall in love with the *person*, not the fantasy.

In cases of 'love at first sight', or at least 'gut' reactions, the primal urge to improve the gene pool kicks in and that's when you react strongly and physically to the possibility of mating with Mr Tall-Strong-Powerful-and-Respected. He's probably perfect for a hot love affair, but if you assume he's 'the one' for a long-term commitment you may be bitterly disappointed. If you're tempted to project your fantasies onto this man (who presumably embodies everything you've ever wanted), there's a good possibility he'll turn out to be a miserable failure of a lover who also doesn't meet any of your other needs. Sound familiar?

If you like someone, but there are no initial fireworks, it might be worth taking Tucker's advice. She says that unless someone is rude, crude, or physically repulsive, it's best to reserve judgement until after three dates. That gives both parties enough time to look beyond superficial qualities, get past unreliable indicators of 'type', and uncover the other person's best qualities.[8] The relationship may take longer to build up to an intense heat, but because it's based on reality (rather than primal urges or projected fantasies), it just might last. You may even find yourself falling head over heels in love *and* lust!

Must-Squash-Attitude No. 6: 'I'm Doomed if I Don't Find Love'

Are you sick of everyone from your mother to the lady you just met on the bus giving you that 'knowing' look and asking when you're going to 'settle down'? If so much clucking and tut-tutting is wearing you down, there's every chance you're well suited to being single. Maybe you don't really need a partner at all, at least full-time. Trouble is, even if you're a totally blissed-out single, everyone else will assume you must be unhappy. Tebbel says 'It's wrong to assume that you've got to be coupled off like animals in the ark to be content.'[9] Just take a good look at the married people around you and you'll soon realise that being in a relationship doesn't necessarily produce lasting happiness.

Do you delight in the prospect of having the whole bed to yourself on a lazy Sunday morning? Do you enjoy being able to come and go as you please, without having to answer to anyone? Would you love to paint the bathroom any colour you want, without a lengthy negotiation? If you answered, yes, yes and yes, maybe you really are (or would be) happier on your own.

According to Dr Fiona Papps, it's time to move beyond the single stereotype. She says there's great pressure on women not to be single and our worth is still judged by our ability to attract a man.[10] Relationships can make some people happy, they can also be miserable beyond belief. If you're single and unhappy, you can change that by looking closely at yourself. As *Cosmopolitan*'s Tracey Cox says, happy singles are the ones who get all the dates.[11] You may still dream of finding true love — there's nothing wrong with that. But in the meantime, try to find some happiness on your own terms.

TRUE TALES...

I know I'm not classically beautiful, but I still get plenty of dates. When I'm at a party, I make an effort to catch a bloke's eyes and smile. Sometimes I even say hello. If someone approaches me, I always give him the time of day, even if he doesn't have much 'dating potential'. (I like to have a laugh.) Some of the 'dishy' blokes I meet start by eyeing off the gorgeous skinny chick in the corner, but they go home with my phone number.

Karen, 28

Must-Squash-Attitude No 7: 'I'm Desperate For Love'

In her book, *The Great Aussie Soulmate Search*, Jordan Kelly says, 'The desire for love, and a soul mate or partner, is still the most fundamental emotional need for most adult humans.'[12] So, why is admitting that you want love so embarrassing?

I mean just look at the title of this book. Would you dare to read it if was about love and not *lurve*? Have you already covered it in brown paper? If not, you run the risk of looking *desperate*, of being *needy*. STOP! What's wrong with wanting to

FINDING ... love with attitude

fulfil your basic human needs? As any first-year psychology student knows, love and belonging are only a little lower down the scale than our need for food and shelter. Sills admits to feeling angry with those who assume that longing for a relationship is a sign of weakness. She believes love is at a woman's centre because we are wise enough to want to live there: with men and without apology.[13]

Let's face it, bagging men is great fun! We know we're more evolved, more complex, nothing short of goddesses; some men even agree. But bagging our *need* for men can be just as bad as bagging ourselves. (And we wouldn't want to do that now, would we?)

Being 'needy' when you're already in a relationship is a different matter; it could be a sign of low self-esteem. Tucker suggests that if you become a wimp when you're with someone you care about, you're too dependent on others for your identity.[14] (For more on self-esteem issues, see: Chapter 6, 'Finding ... love with baggage'.)

Must-Squash-Attitude No. 8: 'I Already Know That ...'

If you're such a know-it-all and positive that you'll never meet anyone anywhere, anytime, do yourself a favour and open your mind to new opportunities. Who knows, you could find the person you're meant to share your life with (or at least a saucy weekend) where you least expect it. So, be flexible.

Maybe you're the type of woman who makes up her mind about something before it happens? You know, that a party will be boring as soon as the invitation arrives. Call it vibes, visualisation, a self-fulfilling prophecy, or stupidity. Because, if you start out being negative you'll usually be right. You've got to open more than just your mind, you've got to open all of yourself (well, perhaps not your legs, at this stage).

Begin by opening your eyes. Believe it or not, there really

are men everywhere; you've just got to be on the look out. Chances are, if you take the time to notice someone he might even notice you back. In fact, he probably has, but because you've got your blinkers on, you didn't realise it.

TRUE TALES....

Once when I was out with my husband and a single girlfriend, I noticed a good-looking bloke giving her the full 'looking-her-up-and-down-with-lust' treatment. While holding hands with hubby, I had a good perve myself. Later I nudged my friend and asked what she thought of the guy who'd been checking her out. She just looked at me and said, 'What guy?' I can't believe she didn't notice him. If I'd been single, I'd have given him my number.

Kayleen, 34

Sometimes not noticing a potential squeeze is due to preconceived ideas about where you're likely to find love. For instance, if you're going to a friend's house for a girls' night in you won't be expecting a single man to knock at the door. (Unless he's the stripper.) But it's been known to happen, and the woman with her eyes open has the best chance of seeing him.

TRUE TALES....

I was at a friend's Tupperware Party and everyone was eating and talking ferociously. The doorbell rang and my friend's husband answered it. Looking down the hallway, I noticed that he was chatting with a guy. They chatted for a few minutes, and the guy had a good look at the room full of gorgeous women before they both headed for the pub.

A few minutes later someone asked the hostess who the guy was. It turns out that she and I were the only ones to notice his arrival — and we were both already married! I thought at the time, a 'decent bloke' just happens to call around, yet the women who should be looking are closed for business. No wonder they're still single. Then again, maybe I'm just an old perve!

Dianna, 38

FINDING ... love with attitude

You might be getting a little over-ambitious if you think you'll meet Mr Right at a Tupperware party. (You're more likely to meet a walrus or two; they like a tight seal!) But Dianna's story illustrates that anything is possible. Is she right in thinking that blinkers are responsible for some women being single? Or, maybe the single women at the Tupperware party were just too busy burping their containers to notice a mere male.

Unless you live in an isolated community, men *are* all around you — you just have to train yourself to spot as many as you can. Go 'shopping' with a friend and turn it into a competition. But beware: you may become so good at it that when you *do* end up partnered you can't break the habit.

Must-Squash-Attitude No. 9: 'I Intimidate Men'

Are you successful, rich, vivacious, assertive, attractive, accomplished ... perhaps all of the above? If so, some men may find you intimidating, but not all. There are men who enjoy wooing a successful, powerful woman so give them a go. Perhaps you've been relying too much on the 'gut' reaction and only dating men you find immediately desirable. But if they're too much like you, they may see you as a threat. Or, their bravado may be masking a lack of self-confidence.

Maybe you never get far enough to even get a date? Either way, believing you intimidate men won't improve your chances. According to clinical psychologist Ayala Malach Pines, a self-fulfilling prophecy can sabotage the initiation stages of a relationship. She says that our behaviour influences the people around us to the extent that 'if a woman treats a "lesser" man as competent, it will bring out his competencies.'[15] Gender stereotypes also play a part. Pines says that when people place a high degree of importance on being accepted by others they can feel pressure to behave according to gender-role stereotypes. Because powerful career women don't always fit the feminine stereotype (you'll find them listed under 'Ball-breaking Bitch'), you may be worrying that your success is what's turning men off. Pines says studies suggest otherwise, and that when the traits most desired by men and women in a partner are examined, there are no gender differences!

So, instead of worrying that you don't conform to the feminine stereotype, do something about it. That doesn't mean putting on a frilly floral frock and fluttering your eyelids. It *does* mean thinking about whether your behaviour is perpetuating a self-fulfilling prophecy during the crucial stages of a relationship. What is it that seems to be scaring those mere males? Is it your powerful personality? There's certainly nothing wrong with that, but it pays to be careful about how you use that power. Especially if you're trying to control the situation to the point where you actually demolish any hope of a long-term affair. Remember: relationships involve more than one person, so don't push people away by appearing so independent that it seems as if you don't need anyone else. Instead, use your power to bring out the best in people.

If you're simply not meeting any men, then maybe you're intimidating because you've closed the door on communication. You might be the most gorgeous woman in the world, but if you're giving off 'not open for inspection' vibes, every man in the room will make a beeline for the woman who's smiling and chatty. On the other hand, maybe the only guys you *do* date are only those cocky enough to penetrate your superior exterior, which means the genuinely nice guy will probably give up after your first disinterested glance.

Smile and make eye contact. An open, friendly face is an extremely powerful way to attract people. Granted, sometimes being too friendly means you get lumbered with the wrong kinds of people. But as Aunt Lurvinya would say, 'You can't sort the weeds from the flowers until you've sown all the seeds!' Or learn from one of Tucker's experiments: she set her students the task of smiling at 50 men in a week. One clever woman cheated, standing at the finishing line of a marathon and smiling at every man who crossed it. She married one of the runners![16]

In the dating game, it's best not to take yourself too seriously. Too many first dates start and end with one or both parties rattling off their 'wish list'. If that's you, no wonder men are intimidated! Take an interest in him, not what he can do for you, or where the relationship is going. It's just a date for goodness sake, not a binding contract. So, relax and start with some small talk. Be up-front about your feelings, but also give yourself time to find out if he's a potential partner before you put down a deposit on the reception hall.

TRUE TALES.... *I don't get asked out much. I don't know why, I'm not ugly or anything. I suppose they must think I already have a boyfriend or something. Someone once told me I was a snob, maybe it's true.*
Tara, 25

6. FINDING.... love with baggage

Dear Aunt Lurvinya,

Not long ago my partner of three years left me. It's not the first time I've found myself single after a long-term relationship. Deep down I know I would still love to meet a man who could make me happy, but I just don't know if I can face going down that track again. I'm carrying enough baggage from past relationships already: lost faith, smashed dreams and a great big broken heart. Right now all I feel like doing is getting my own back on my ex and hurting him like he hurt me. Got any ideas?

Ms Ribble

Dear Ms Ribble,

So, you thought you'd met Mr Right and things went terribly wrong — again. Your friends tell you you'll get over him, that time will heal. You know it's probably true, but you just can't seem to climb out of that black hole. Your mum says you'll find someone more deserving, but how can you even think of going through all that again? Especially if you're still in love with the double-bastard, dog-faced pig. If you want revenge, how about voodoo? Stick a pin right in the effigy of your 'effing' ex so he can find out just how much your heart is hurting. Personally, I prefer simply popping a couple of prawns in his car heater or curtain rails. Come summer, you won't be accused of hanging around like a bad smell but something will be getting up his nose.

You are seeing revenge as a way of restoring your self-respect. He hurt you and left you feeling powerless. Giving him the raw prawn may make you feel better but only for a few minutes. What you really need to do is show him how fabulous your life is without him. He may have been relegated to the 'enemy' camp, but as long as you're engaging with him, somebody's having a relationship. Time to take back the power and turn your life around. Show him that he can't hurt you any more. You may need professional help and time, but those suitcases you're carting around will eventually feel much lighter, and travelling through life may even become a pleasure.

Aunt Lurvinya

Have You Overpacked?

Only newborn babies come with a clean slate. By the time the rest of us have made it through the agonies of adolescent acne, we have a past — good, bad or indifferent. Some of us have to cope with death, disease and divorce before we're emotionally ready to cope with more than waking up with a zit the size of a small volcano on the morning of a deb ball. If these problems or issues go unresolved, they can prevent you from leading a full and satisfying life. Instead of feeling positive about the future, you're only partly happy or downright miserable, always on the lookout for another monster lurking in the shadows. Perhaps that's why some people in love relationships claim they 'can't get no satisfaction'?

In order to make satisfying attachments, we need to overcome inner barriers. As Sills says, 'weak selves make desperate attachments; hungry selves make cloying, annoying ones. Frightened selves withhold love. Dependent selves make demands.'[1] If you're weak, hungry, frightened or dependent it's likely that unresolved issues are holding you back. These manifest themselves in some pretty heavy baggage. But Sills says that understanding your baggage and taking steps to minimise what you're carrying around can make 'life easier, sweeter, and richer in opportunity ... '[2] It's all about making love more accessible. You may still experience irritations and disillusionment from time to time, but you'll find them easier to bear.

So let's take a closer look inside the suitcases some of us might be lugging around.

Bag No. 1: A Broken Heart

This is a heavy one, but you haven't really lived until you've had a broken heart. If you haven't reached the stage where time has healed all wounds, log on to a website like *aboutyourbreakup.com*, where you can chat away with others in the same situation and get plenty of ideas to help heal your broken heart.

What about contacting your local white witch for a couple of spells to fix things or visiting a psychic? You could do worse than reciting this affirmation:

> Today I'll take a closer look at the qualities I admired about my ex. Today I'll try to develop those same qualities in myself.[3]

Could he wiggle his penis up and down with no hands? Well, that's an admirable talent, if anatomically impossible for you to imitate. How about his talent for deception? Hmm … maybe not. Just because he slept with your best friend doesn't mean you have to stoop to his level.

The truth is, none of these quick-fix suggestions are much use. Relationship counsellors say that losing a partner through separation or divorce can be as devastating as a death. In fact, sometimes it can be worse. Because if 'the ex' is alive and well someone else can have him. Even if you don't want him anymore, the sight of him with another woman can produce powerful feelings of jealousy. Just as people who've experienced the death of a loved one need time to grieve, you should also give yourself time to work through your loss before moving on.

In their book, *When Your Lover Leaves You*, Richard G. Whiteside and Frances E. Steinberg, record the stages of grief:

1. Shock — everything closes down, we feel numb, our eating and sleeping patterns are up the creek, we may even feel physically ill or turn into a raving hysterical madwoman.
2. Hope — we fantasise about getting back together and attempt reconciliation, sometimes promising to change.

3. Anger — we feel furious about how we have been treated, and our goal becomes revenge.
4. Despair — we are tormented by our shortcomings; feel unloved and unworthy, even depressed. The temptation is to cut ourselves off from the world.
5. Indifference — we are able to put things into perspective and establish our identity as a separate person who has the strength and ability to satisfy our own needs. We are ready to move on.
6. Growth — all doubts of self worth are diminished and we have come to terms with our loss.[4]

Not everyone experiences every symptom or in the same order. You may lock yourself in your bedroom for a week before you decide to run a nail file down the side of his custom-built ute. But to truly heal, you'll need to move through each stage. When I interviewed social psychologist, Dr Julie Fitness, she said it's important to remember that the intensity of your emotions *will* fade over time. Recognise that what you're experiencing is a process that needs to be *worked* through. Having a close friend to talk to can help, but beware of boring everyone to death with your tales of woe. If you get stuck in that stage, seek professional help from someone who can help you explore your emotions objectively, in context and with a big box of tissues close at hand.[5]

Believe it or not, it helps to think about your own contribution to the breakdown. You see, although 'the ex' is definitely a bastard-pig (we all agree on that one), the break-up may not be entirely his fault. Green says that when relationships break down there's something defective about the way both parties relate.[6] Thinking about your behaviour will give you a measure of control that can help you avoid making the same mistakes in the future. Your role in the break-up may not even have anything to do with direct actions, but rather the baggage you've been carting around from past relationships.

It takes time, but you will be able to open that battered suitcase again. The contents may have shifted — no more anger, despair, or silly thoughts of revenge. Even better, the inner strength you never knew you had, the friends who supported you in the darkest hours, and the resolutions based on past mistakes, may even mean that your heart won't be in two pieces for very long. You'll probably even use the contents to ensure the success of future relationships.

Bag No. 2: The Past

Unresolved issues from childhood can range from devastating trauma or abuse, to things you just can't put your finger on. All can affect your quest for love. No matter what end of the spectrum your experiences sit, unless you deal with them it can cause you to choose the wrong man again and again.

Green explains this 'patterning' in the light of (or absence of) a relationship with your father (or another key parental figure). The way you relate to Dad can set the tone for how you relate to men in your intimate relationships. For instance, sometimes meeting a new man is like having a second chance to seek the approval, love, respect and conflict-free relationship you didn't have with Dad during your childhood. Trouble is, if you haven't yet resolved your issues with him, this 'second chance' will be just as fruitless.

Another reason women may choose men like their father is an attempt to gain control over something that happened during childhood. If you actively choose men who abuse, abandon, cheat, or disrespect you, then they're still the ones with all the control. You may not suffer to the same degree as in childhood, but you'll probably never be happy either.

But Dad can't take all the blame. Hollonds says all intimate relationships have similarities to the parent/child relationship. If you were hurt, or your needs weren't met at any stage in your life, it might take a lot of life experience to get over that. Similarly, if you idealise the relationship you had with a parent or anyone else during your formative years, it may represent something that you've lost and you may spend the rest of your life searching for a replacement.[7]

CYNDI KAPLAN-FREIMAN'S TIPS ON 'HOW TO STOP PICKING UP THE WRONG MAN'

Make sure ...

He doesn't need to be saved

He isn't driven by wild ambition

He isn't totally macho

He isn't wildly handsome

He doesn't need help finding himself

He doesn't drink, gamble, or argue too much

He isn't married

Then ask yourself: 'Am I in love or in pain?'[8]

Carrying negative emotions from one relationship to the next can affect all your relationships. Fitness says unresolved anger, jealousy and anxiety can colour the way we look at the world. We watch our new partner for danger signals and the minute we see (or think we see) one, we overreact. 'We need to deal with these emotions if we are to have successful relationships in the future — and it might mean seeking professional help,' she says.[9] It certainly means resisting the urge to jump straight into a new relationship without dealing with the shit from the one before!

The difficulty with baggage is that because we don't react to it on a conscious level it's often hard to recognise when it affects our relationships. It may be helpful to ask yourself questions about continuing patterns in your relationships. Read the profiles below and see if you recognise anyone. If you suspect you have unresolved issues, then getting professional advice is the best and fastest way of moving forward.

BLAST FROM THE PAST!

If these stories ring true, it's time to ...

Mena's boyfriend is talking to an attractive girl at a party. She feels her skin turning red then green. How could he do this to her when he knows that her ex did the dirty? She disappears into the loo with a box of tissues and wonders if it is all over.

Angie was ten when her Dad left. When she was 20, her boyfriend left. At 30, her husband walked out. Now 35, Angie's in love with Ivan. He's not the marrying kind; he's told her so. She knows he'll leave her eventually. They always do. When he does, she'll say, 'I knew it.'

Donna spent five years with Mr Tightarse. They were saving for a house and he blew his stack if she spent money on new clothes. Greg is her latest love. In a shop, he whistles at the price tag on a dress she's thinking of buying. Donna tosses the dress back on the rack and storms out of the shop. For the rest of the day, Greg gets the silent treatment.

When Zadie's parents spilt up, her Mum spent hours telling everyone how useless her Dad was. As she grew up, Zadie began to see it for herself. Even now, her upper lip curls into a sneer whenever she thinks of her Dad. It's a sneer that Zadie's boyfriend Jerome knows all too well. He's been called a *@#*wit, an idiot and a useless bastard. She doesn't always tell him to his face, preferring to mutter under her breath. Jerome puts up with it, but there's only so much he can take, everyone needs a bit of self-respect.

Tina never went 'all the way' with her first boyfriend, but she did have her first orgasm while heavy petting in his car (something to do with the gear stick). She's in her thirties now and the blokes she meets just don't 'do it' for her. She often suggests going parking, but the one bloke who agreed drove an automatic.

When she was a child, Karen's Dad called her 'His Little Princess'. He gave her everything she wanted and pandered to her every whim. When her boyfriend Ian asked her not to shave her legs with his razor, she threw herself on the bed and wailed; if he really loved her, he would want to share everything, wouldn't he?

FINDING SELF

Bag No. 3: Low Self-Esteem

Low self-esteem can severely hamper your search for love. If, deep down, you don't think yourself worthy enough to find happiness and love, you'll never establish realistic relationships. Instead, you'll settle for men who can only bring unhappiness, or accept behaviour that makes you unhappy. Either way, the relationship is doomed.

You may believe you need love to complete yourself because you're not already happy within. You think that if the right man would only come along you'd be a better person, could lose weight, be more organised, get your life on track. Or, the reverse may be true: as soon as you get your boobs done, lose weight, blah, blah, blah … you'll meet the man of your dreams. It's a form of procrastinating or 'putting off' anything you can't imagine achieving through your own strength of character.

We spend our lives trying to become more complete, more fulfilled, but perhaps in the quest to find the great love of our life, we're really seeking to speed up the process of becoming whole? We often hear people who are in love say things like, 'It's as if I've met my other half' or 'I feel whole.' But it's a mistake to rely on the love of a man (or anyone else) to make you complete. Surely, you should be striving to do that yourself, in your way. And if that wonderful man of your dreams should drop by, the more the merrier.

Sometimes you've got to put your search for love on hold and examine your life in detail. A bit of navel gazing can help you discover unhealthy aspects of your personality that you can repair before they get out of control. If you hate your job, home, financial situation, friends and family, find out why and make some changes. It's your life and it's in your hands. Taking control will help you feel happier and that will be reflected in the way you behave.

Once you're happier with your life, you'll be more attractive to other people including potential 'lurve matches'! As Tucker says, 'the happier you are with your life, the more likely it is that someone will want to become a part of it. When you are turned on about yourself, other people are turned on to you.'[10] Becoming aware of your own talents, gifts, strengths and weaknesses will help you like yourself inside and out. If you don't, no one else will.

TRUE TALES...
I can spend ages getting ready to go out and look really good. But because I'm feeling down, I don't get chatted up. On the other hand, there have been times when I've looked like a dog, but men flocked to me because I was in a good mood. I reckon it's got a lot to do with how I'm feeling about myself. If I know I'm fab, I'm fab!
Suzanne, 33

Lack of self-esteem not only undermines relationships, it can turn you into a convenient doormat. As Kaplan-Freiman says, 'no one can walk all over you unless you lie down and allow yourself to be trampled'.[11] Boundaries are hard to change, but don't wait to seek help if you're in a love relationship where you're oppressed or co-dependent. If you still can't successfully reset the boundaries, it might be time to consider getting out. That step often takes the greatest courage of all.

For some, low self-esteem manifests itself in shyness. Some people are simply reserved, which is a personality trait, not a problem. It's only if shyness is holding you back that you need to do something about it. In the lurve game, being shy might mean it's difficult for you to engage with people you don't know very well. However, if it's been years since you got smoochy with anyone other than your family or a furry friend, it might be time to give shyness the old heave-ho.

You can overcome shyness and other self-esteem issues by taking an assertiveness course or changing bad mental habits. For example, if someone compliments you on that great report, delicious cake or hand-painted plate don't mutter, 'Well, I had a lot of help' before pointing out the mistakes no one can see but you. Don't assume they're 'just being nice'. Instead, say, 'Thank you very much', and give yourself a pat on the back. There's nothing wrong with acknowledging your strengths. Accepting that someone else thinks you're terrific may help you believe the same thing!

Hollonds suggests a two-step strategy to overcome shyness. First, start safe by doing things that make you feel good about yourself. That might mean a hobby, a course, or a new sport. Anything you enjoy. Then stretch yourself with a new interest or put yourself in a situation that makes you feel challenged. You may need to take a friend initially, but as you begin to push past your boundaries, you'll begin to feel more capable.[12] Widening your circle of friends is always a self-esteem booster. Everyone feels good when someone takes an interest, which can stimulate behaviour that is even more daring.

Bag No. 4: Fear

FEAR OF BEING ALONE

Cosmopolitan's Tracey Cox is deeply suspicious of people who've never been single. 'If you've always got someone hanging off your arm then how do you learn to stand on your own two feet?'[13] Similarly, if you continue to form relationships with men who are emotionally unavailable, need fixing, have addictions or other emotional problems and issues, it's time to spend some time alone. While you're enjoying your own company, make a conscious decision to be more selective in your choice of future mates. Because, until you understand what motivates you, chronic heartbreak will be your destiny.

According to a good friend, some single American women are going so public with their decision to be alone that they're marrying themselves! They're wearing white gowns, reciting vows and even throwing showers to help with the costs of setting up a new home. Regardless of what they get up to on their 'wedding night', these women are clear about one thing: they're still open to a love relationship with a man. They're simply letting the world know that they're also happy alone, thank you very much.

It's not always easy. Coming home to an empty house can be physically and emotionally painful. That's why so many of us would rather endure an unsatisfying relationship than spend time in our own company. Strategies for overcoming this type of loneliness are not as difficult as they seem. For instance, you don't have to start babbling to yourself to fill the silence (although there's nothing wrong with that). It's more a matter of finding out how to fill in all the hours.

Why not be completely self-indulgent: eat a carton of ice cream while watching chick flicks, buy a dog, write a book! The world is your oyster. And, who knows, you might just find a pearl. Discover what you really like doing and you'll be itching to get home to finish knitting that angora jumper or building that solar-powered car. When you do feel like company, join an amateur theatre group, or volunteer at your local hospital. There's nothing like helping others to make you realise how lucky you are.

There are a lot of happy single people in the world (they just don't get enough publicity). With a little effort, you too can join their ranks instead of relying on others to complete your life and make you blissfully happy. Some of the loneliest people are those who are abused, trapped, or simply not connected to their partners. Isn't it better to be happily on your own than with someone out of boredom or fear? That way, if you find yourself in a relationship and he comes home, turns on the TV and grunts, you'll have better company to keep yourself occupied: your own.

TRUE TALES...

After breaking up from my childhood sweetheart of nine years, I went through a stage of looking for another partner. But I became totally disillusioned with the games men play and went from one unsuccessful interlude to the next.

When people asked me when I was going to meet Mr Right, I felt very defensive. I hated that whole 'blind date' thing and thought my married matchmaker friends were being smug. Once I went to counselling, I realised that they were just trying to help.

Seeing my therapist has really helped me work through my issues and now I feel happy with my life and myself. I even concluded that a partner is not essential for my happiness.

That's when I met my husband!

Justine, 34

FEAR OF REJECTION

No one likes rejection. A blow to the ego feels like crap, and, while some people can brush themselves off and get on with it, it's not always that easy. A big blow can be so soul destroying that you subconsciously put yourself in a position where rejection can't reach you. In other words, you fall in love with unattainable men who can never reject you. He might be someone out of your league, he might be married. Whoever he is, when you set your sights on him, you're using a protection strategy; seeking unrequited love is far less painful than taking a chance on real rejection. If the implausible happens, and he leaves Hollywood (*and* Jennifer Aniston) for you, chances are you won't want him anymore. After all, how could you live with someone with such bad taste?

Time to toughen up. If you're going to start looking for love, you're going to have to face up to rejection. Not everyone will love or even like you — it's a statistical impossibility! The trick is, don't take it personally. If someone doesn't want to go on another date with you or fails to respond to your chat-up line, they're not necessarily rejecting you as a person. Maybe they're happy being single, or hard of hearing! Whatever the reason, you can guarantee it's not *your* fault.

Eventually, if you take enough risks you'll find someone compatible who genuinely wants to spend time getting to know you. You may not find the love of your life, but you could find a new best friend. Drop your guard and let someone into your life and you may even hear yourself say, 'Gee, he must have very good taste to be with someone like me!'

That's not to say that you'll never be hurt again. Linda Georgian, author of *How To Attract your Ideal Mate*, says that having a relationship involves emotional risk and part of that is being willing to get hurt.[14] You don't have to throw yourself to the lions; sometimes it's better to keep your true feelings to yourself until you're sure they're reciprocated. But at least going out on a limb gives you the chance to applaud yourself for not falling off.

TRUE TALES...

I had been going out with a guy I really liked for a month or so. Then he went away for a couple of weeks. The weekend he was due back, I was so frightened he wouldn't call that I turned off my phone. If I'd left it on, I would have spent the whole time obsessing. On Monday, I turned it back on and there was a message waiting!

Carolyn, 26

FEAR OF BEING LOVED

The emotional disclosure required in intimate relationships can be both exciting and frightening. Judith Sills says that, for some women, nothing can seem more dangerous than 'settling'.[15] The thought of yielding or perhaps becoming submissive makes them feel weak and they fear being overwhelmed by men.

Laura Doyle, author of *The Surrendered Wife,* disagrees, saying a woman's mantra must become 'surrender' if marriage is to work.[16] With such conflicting advice, it's no surprise that so many of us are scared witless! These kind of self-help books may contain *some* useful ideas for *some* people, but most do nothing to quell every fear. Besides, changing your personality to please a man is not what good loving is all about. Sills says achieving satisfying love relationships isn't about becoming the person he wants you to be. However, she suggests that if you become the person *you* want to be, one of the rewards will be love.[17] Yes, you will give up a great deal to maintain a successful relationship. But it can be well worth all the effort, otherwise why would anybody bother!

QUIZ

Answer the questions in our fun quiz to discover if you are ... A Sex Kitten or a Scaredy Cat

1. At a party full of pretty women, a great looking guy makes a beeline for you. You ...
   a) think that someone has paid him to talk to you as a joke so you turn red and dash to the loo.
   b) think the lucky charm you have in your pocket must be working.
   c) smile and dazzle him with your fantastic personality.

FINDING SELF

2   The last time you had a boyfriend your Mum ...
    a)   welcomed him into the family.
    b)   fainted from shock.
    c)   called him by the wrong name and asked you to stick with blokes named David so she could keep up.

3   Your flatmates are away for the weekend and your friends are all busy. You ...
    a)   watch a bit of TV, do a few chores and have a rotten time.
    b)   phone a friend you haven't seen for ages (because she gets on your nerves) and arrange a night out.
    c)   enjoy the silence and use up all the hot water in a long bath.

4   The last bloke you were madly in love with was ...
    a)   Russell Crowe.
    b)   someone you met at a party.
    c)   married.

5   There's a cute guy who's always at the coffee shop where you buy lunch. He starts dropping hints about having a Friday night drink. You ...
    a)   start buying your sandwiches elsewhere.
    b)   tell him it's a good idea but never make arrangements.
    c)   fix a time and a place.

6   The guy you've been seeing starts making noises about getting more serious. You ...
    a)   feel your heart miss a beat; this could be love!
    b)   suddenly notice that he picks his fingernails and dribbles while eating his cornflakes. How could you live with *that*?
    c)   groan; you're quite happy with the way things are.

SCORES

1. $a - 5, b - 3, c - 0$ 2. $a - 0, b - 4, c - 5$ 3. $a - 4, b - 5, c - 0$
4. $a - 5, b - 0, c - 4$ 5. $a - 5, b - 3, c - 0$ 6. $a - 0, b - 5, c - 3$

0–4 Congratulations, Sex Kitten! You're not afraid of anything, especially lurve.

5–15 When it comes to lurve, you can be a bit of a chicken, but when the heart's involved, who isn't? You know you can get hurt but have a go regardless. Stick with it and take a deep breath, you're doing fine.

16–30 Hey, Scaredy Cat! What are you so frightened of? Too many boyfriends or not enough? Come on, if you're not already running from your own shadow you soon will be. If you're looking for lurve, it's time to lay yourself on the line. Okay, you might get hurt. Then again, you might not.

Bag No. 5: Inability to Give Love

How do you get the loving right? Stephanie Dowrick says the first step is being able to tell the difference between self-love and self-absorption. Being egocentric and selfish can interfere with your love relationships as much as low self-esteem. It may seem like the most normal thing in the world to put your interests first, but as Dowrick maintains: 'the happiest people among us are also the most altruistic. These are the people who value their own existence and can give to others without strain.'[18] It's the basis of most ancient spiritual teachings and still rings true. How many of you are on a fast track to self-fulfilment; thinking and speaking in the singular, measuring everything in terms of your own success and what it can do for you? True self-love comes from recognising how your life overlaps with, and reflects the lives of others.

That's the road to happiness and it's something most psychologists — pop or otherwise — agree on. Yet, so many of us just can't seem to get it. Of course, the tendency to become 'me' centred is especially prevalent when you are hurting, needy, lonely, or grieving. When that happens, it's common to hear yourself saying, '*I'm* the one hard done by,' '*I* deserve better,' '*I* want what she's got,' and 'Why does this always happen to *me*?' Sound familiar? While these statements may all be true, when they're put before everything and everyone else it can cause great unhappiness.

According to Sills, love is about giving, whereas need focuses on receiving.[19] Love shouldn't be about what you're going to get out of a relationship or what the other person is going to 'do for you'. This is true in any relationship, not just with men. Are you in the habit of giving to your friends, your family and your lovers? Or, do you always do the taking? And, if so, does it make you happy?

In his article 'Mirror, Mirror', Dr Bruce A. Stevens talks about the person who's read dozens of self-help books but still can't find any solace. He says this is because 'what is described is not what you actually experience. It is like a merry-go-round: nothing changes and you cannot get off.'[20] Stevens suggests that although everyone is self-centred to a degree, some people have 'narcissistic' issues that make it impossible for them to find happiness in relationships. This is not to be confused with being selfish, says Stevens. 'A person with narcissistic issues can act in blatantly selfish ways and yet be unaware of his or her degree of self-focus.'[21] A selfish act implies choice, whereas narcissists are unable to recognise the needs of others and are often blind to their own shortcomings. They may be able to function normally, but are rarely satisfied when in a relationship because they exhibit a destructive self-love.

The trouble with 'me' centred people is that they can't recognise their narcissistic tendencies. They may recognise the symptoms — difficult relationships with family, friends and lovers — but they're never to blame, it's always somebody else's fault. To boost his book sales and capture a wider readership, perhaps Dr Stevens should have called his book *Why Isn't Everyone as Great as Me?*

MIRROR, MIRROR ON THE WALL, OF COURSE I'M THE FAIREST OF THEM ALL

QUIZ

Take this quiz to discover if self-love is undermining your relationships.

1   Is someone your hero one minute and your enemy the next? Yes☐ No☐

QUIZ

2 Do you 'lose the plot' if you don't get good service in shops or restaurants? Yes☐ No☐

3 Do you shout, 'people shit me!' from the car while driving? Yes☐ No☐

4 Are you mortally offended when someone criticises you or your work? Yes☐ No☐

5 Do you have trouble seeing where relationships went wrong? Yes☐ No☐

6 Do you find it difficult to accept other people's opinions? Yes☐ No☐

7 Have you 'suffered like no other has suffered' and force others to suffer along with you? Yes☐ No☐

8 Do you sometimes fly into violent or uncontrollable rages? Yes☐ No☐

9 Can you tolerate imperfection in a partner? Yes☐ No☐

10 Are you ruthless? Yes☐ No☐

11 Do you feel you are special or unique, yet also harbour bad feelings about yourself? Yes☐ No☐

12 Are you obsessed with your appearance? Yes☐ No☐

13 Do you suffer from an aching hunger (for food, sex, booze, love, or something you can't put your finger on) that is never fully satisfied? Yes☐ No☐

How did you go?

If you answered yes to three or more questions, then your bad behaviour is the result of more than just a bad day. Perhaps it's time to take a good, long look in the mirror, or stop looking so much. You just might be your own worst enemy. Time to buy a copy of Dr Stevens' book or seek professional help. What are you waiting for?

Sills says that people with a sense of superiority reassure themselves of their high personal standing by pointing out how others fall short. However, underneath that constant criticism the perfectionist harbours a secret dread that she's not that special. She envies others and insists on excellence before bestowing her love and approval. In short, she's a hard woman to love.[22] At the other end of the scale are people who make themselves 'loveable' by becoming human doormats.

Finding a balance between the two is about strengthening your own capacity to love.

You've missed the point if you only increase your capacity to give love for a trade-off; you have to be genuinely open. By creating a more serene spirit within, you can become a person who is easier to love. Instead of asking, 'What is this going to get me?' try, 'Where can this take me?'[23]

Linda Georgian says, 'you must be able to give love to yourself and others, but it is equally important to be able to receive it'.[24] By learning the art of receiving love, you'll discover that a truly loving act is one given without expectations. When someone compliments you, don't apologise or assume they'll expect you to return the compliment. The same goes when someone does you a favour; you needn't feel indebted or that you must return it immediately. Just receive it in the spirit in which it was given: as a loving gift. Georgian also says that 'kind words and deeds may be done by people that you barely know'.[25] So, try not to have fixed ideas about how other people give love or you may miss gifts that come from another source.

A Prayer

Dear God,

Today is a good day.

I didn't bitch at my boyfriend or slag-off my boss.

I didn't hide all the chocolate biscuits in my desk and leave the plain ones for everyone else.

I didn't abuse my Mum when she asked if I'm okay.

I didn't even throw anything.

For that, I give thanks.

But the clock is ticking,

And I'm going to have to get out of bed soon,

So from that moment on ...

I'm going to need your help.

AMEN

FINDING ... love with baggage

Bag No. 6: Total Confusion

LOVE AND LUST

Do you rely on a gut reaction to gauge whether you're in love? Is there a possibility that what you think is an attraction might simply be lust? For Simon Andreae, the distinction between love and lust are as different as chalk and cheese. Love, he says, 'may be vital for parental care' but it's not necessary 'for reproduction'.[26]

John Gray expands on that theory when he says, 'there are basically four kinds of chemistry between dating partners: physical, emotional, mental and spiritual ... '[27] It's only when we're attracted to someone in all four ways that love has the potential to be successful. Of course, it's one thing to blame everything on the mind, but our hormones also play an important role in how we're feeling.

For example, the level of testosterone — the aggressive, 'gotta get me some' hormone — increases when women ovulate. Perhaps the fact that it's also the most fertile stage in our cycle explains why that's often when we 'want a bit'. Unfortunately, some of us are conditioned to believe that physical desire is 'naughty' or 'dirty' and that we have to be 'in love' to satisfy our carnal urges.

Many women feel great pressure to be in a committed relationship before they can fully express their sexuality. If more women learned to relax the gender role stereotypes that constitute acceptable behaviour, perhaps they wouldn't feel that commitment was necessary just to have a bit of fun in the sack. And perhaps men wouldn't be so quick to run away.

In *Sacred Pleasure*, Riane Eisler reveals the conditioning behind such views. Sex, says Eisler, was once regarded as a sacred act and because we've 'been taught to think of sex as sinful, dirty, titillating or prurient, the thought that sex could be spiritual, much less sacred, is shocking'.[28] Hmmm ... how much easier would it be (not to mention more fun) if we could think about our desire for sex as something beautiful and magical; an indication of a long-repressed impulse toward a more spiritual and more intensely passionate means of expressing love?

Unfortunately, thanks to the long-standing doctrines of some powerful and puritanical regimes, sex has had a bad rap. Before the days when humans worshiped one or more male gods, there were loads of goddesses (like Venus) who had men in awe of their sexuality. But that admiration soon turned to fear, and fear to repression. And in the 19th century, it wasn't uncommon for women with what is now considered a normal sex drive to be hospitalised for nymphomania!

Thankfully, we've come a long way since then. Or have we? In spite of the fact that sex has come out of the closet, old habits die hard. And too many women still deny their primal urges in order to preserve their 'reputation'. In the back of our minds, we still believe the hoary old chestnut that women who have sex without love are cheap.

But it's not women who are cheap — it's sex. It's so everywhere it's in danger of becoming overrated. Is this because we're so inundated with media sex scenes — not to mention pornography — that all the magic is gone? For Greer, pornography is the 'sex' of the millennium. She describes its popularity as, 'the flight from woman, men's denial of sex as a medium of communication ... '[29] Maybe we're just confused by an innate yearning to rediscover the magic; we want sex to be mystical, passionate and powerful. To fully communicate with men on that level, we must imagine ourselves 'in love' and open more than just our legs.

If you've managed to separate your physical desire for sex from your emotions, and are happily pursuing your needs without guilt (even the subconscious variety), bravo! But if your physical urges are tangled up in how you feel about a man, maybe it's time to put on the brakes. Casual sex is great, if that's what you both want. If you're feeling vulnerable, make sure you both know what you're getting into before slipping between the sheets. Or, as the long-suffering Dorothy once advised in *Men Behaving Badly*, don't let his willy wear your nice 'pink anorak' until you're sure of his intentions.

Do you like him as a person? Does he make you feel good about yourself? Do you enjoy being with him? Are you attracted intellectually and spiritually? Are you in love or in lust? Once you've got that sorted, go for it, girl!

IN LOVE WITH LOVE

Often confusion can result not so much from physical urges, but from our inability to deal with our emotions. Too often, we're simply in love with the idea of 'being in love'. Get the picture? You're so desperate to be swept away that you're head-over-heels at the first sign of attraction. People even tell you that you fall in love too easily. Well, maybe they're right. How many times have you met someone, imagined that you'd fallen in love and started behaving like someone in love? Then, within a few weeks or months, you're tired of him because he hasn't lived up to your expectations? Were you really *in love* or just horny?

An eagerness to fall in love can often make the most ridiculous coincidences seem like a sign from heaven that a relationship was 'meant to be'. 'Ohmygod! We-both-love-anchovy-and-peanut butter-sandwiches. He must be *the one*.' During the attraction stage, a man only has the potential to be a dreamboat; he still has to prove himself. Which is why projecting your fantasies onto someone else can be a recipe for disaster. But your willingness to fall in love also could be a yearning for a spiritual experience, especially if you neglect that side of yourself.

We live in a secular society; church attendance is dropping and, for many, it's embarrassing to admit to a fondness for traditional faith or prayer. It's far more socially acceptable to pursue the dozens of 'New Age' spiritual paths, because there's usually no risk if you decide to chop and change. (No one's likely to be excommunicated from a yoga class.) But where does that leave those people who want to explore a deep spiritual yearning? Well, many people who desire to connect with something larger than themselves — with the universe, the land, God, Buddha, Allah, or a Native American Chief — are trying to fill a spiritual void. Some may even try to fill that void with a mere mortal man. Sex *can* be spiritual and can connect two (or more) people in ways that can't compare with most other forms of communication. It can also be fun on your own! For some enlightened women, heaven is a vibrator with fresh batteries! So, if you're after spiritual fulfilment, don't look for it in a casual bonk.

Don't know where to start? Well, you could try a clergyperson, a psychic, even colonic irrigation! Or, forget about the experts and become your own guru: map out a personal spiritual path by choosing from a range of spiritual teachings that correspond with your aims in life.

Not Knowing What You Want

Do you have a clear idea of why you want a love relationship and what you want to get out of it, or are you still blindly rushing in hoping whoever crosses your path wants the same things you do? Well, if divorce statistics are anything to go by, you're not alone. Too many couples, it seems, are prepared to make one of life's most momentous decisions without first discussing or resolving vital issues. Things like children and how to bring them up. Or religion, money and politics. Papps aptly dubs these omissions 'potential minefields'. So, forget about trying to 'read' a man's signals and be open and up-front about what you both want from the start. You don't have to work through a checklist on the first date, just be honest about the type of relationship you hope will develop. It's not about pressure; it's about communication. He can't read your mind any better than you can read his. And if you still imagine that he'll change over time, get real. He may change eventually, but it won't be because of you.

Seeking Help

Relationships Australia has 80 centres around the country offering a range of services, from counselling to courses. Phone: 1300 364 277 or 1800 817 569; www.relationships.com.au

Support groups and other services Contact your local community centre, family health clinic, or GP for information.

Private practitioners Check the Yellow Pages under: 'Counselling — Marriage, Family & Personal'

7. FINDING.... love with kids in tow

Dear Aunt Lurvinya,

The last time I tried dating, it was a disaster. As a single Mum, I can't afford to pay for a babysitter so I decided to invite a guy I liked over for dinner. I set the table with candles and flowers, and even managed to get the kids to bed before he arrived. But while dinner was cooking the little one started crying, and by the time I managed to settle her down the chicken was burnt. We were just getting into dessert and some decent conversation when my eldest said he'd had a nightmare and wanted to sleep in my bed. I put 'Thomas the Tank Engine' in the video to keep him quiet, but my 'date' went home before coffee.

Elle Ofanite

Dear Elle,

Did you know The Teletubbies have a cult following among adults? Apparently, they're great viewing after you get home from a nightclub — something to do with the surreal landscape and Tinky Winky's handbag. However, a romantic dinner for two to the strains of 'Thomas the Tank Engine' isn't quite the same thing, is it?

You've heard the saying 'never mix business with pleasure'; the same rule applies to dating with kids. Your job is to ensure the business end of your life doesn't encroach on finding a bit of pleasure. If you can't afford a babysitter, you'll have to be a bit more resourceful. Tap relatives, neighbours and friends; or organise some reciprocal babysitting to help give other mums and dads a break. That way you can schedule time to nurture your love life without having to nurture your nearest and dearest at the same time. After all, that sort of intimacy can wait until things get far more serious.

Aunt Lurvinya

Single Mums Who Date: The Trade-Off

Most mothers fantasise about being left alone or being able to drop everything for the occasional night on the town with a bunch of friends. Are you guilty of setting up enterprise bargaining agreements with your four-year-old just to get half an hour's uninterrupted silence when you're on the loo? Or, if you want to go out, do you spend half the day making things easier for the person who's agreed to hold the fort in your absence? If you're like most single mothers, a partner to share the workload and provide time to pursue a short path to self-pleasure is a luxury you've probably learned to live without.

If you've suffered a messy relationship break-up or lost a partner through tragic circumstances, you probably don't even have time to wallow in self-pity because staying strong for the sake of the children takes priority. But if you've reached the stage where you'd like to find solace in the arms of another, how do you explain that to a teenage daughter who's just been given a lecture on the importance of getting to know someone before having sex?

Then, of course, there's money to consider or the lack of it. If you don't have supportive relatives willing to provide free babysitting, you can add at least another $50 to the cost of your night out — not to mention the price of coping with energetic children the next morning when your head's full of jackhammers. Even if your dancing shoes have been relegated to the dress-up box and you've decided to take the planned approach to finding love, you still need time and money.

At times, you may envy your single girlfriends even more than the happily married ones, thinking it must be so easy for them to go out and meet interesting men. Then, when you do meet a possible catch and he asks the million-dollar question, 'what do you do?' you watch his eyes glaze over as you answer, 'I'm usually at home looking after the kids'. It's the quickest way to become uninteresting and invisible, yet you're hardly likely to disown the people you love more than anything in the world for the sake of a date.

It might be reassuring to know there are loads of women out there who wish they were in your shoes. Wanting to have children is probably one of the key motivators for women looking for a loving partner. And if the body clock is ticking, they feel even more pressure to find a partner and fast. Over the age of 35, they can see the end in sight. By 40, it's panic stations or making the decision not to have children at all. But it's not just an issue for single women; even those with a partner sometimes sacrifice a desire for children for the sake of an adult relationship.

So, while life can be tough as a single parent, at least you've achieved something many other women aspire to. But balancing the love for your kids with the desire to have a romantic relationship with a man can be tough.

Get Your Priorities Right

Seeking a love relationship when you're a parent comes with buckets of guilt. It's often hard to accept that there's nothing wrong with wanting happiness for yourself as well as your children. But take comfort in the advice of Dr Judy Kuriansky, author of *The Complete Idiot's Guide to Dating*. She says that it's important to fulfil your personal needs because 'your happiness spills over into how you treat your kids'.[1] However, that doesn't necessarily mean the love you feel for your kids and the happiness it generates will spill effortlessly into your love relationships.

Men with children may understand that your kids come first, but sometimes Mr Single-and-Fancy-Free may not like playing second fiddle to someone a third his size. That, however, is something he's going to have to deal with if he falls for you. Be honest and explain the benefits and brickbats of dating a mum. If he can't handle it, let him go. It may hurt, but you're better off finding someone who is prepared to share the joys of children.

Hollonds says that when it comes to introducing a new man into your children's life, it's a wise woman who takes things very slowly. She says children benefit the most from having one-on-one time with their parents. It's when you try to cater for the needs of another adult that you run into trouble. And what's the point of introducing another adult into your child's life if it may not work out? After all, they may become so attached that they'll suffer if it fizzles out. Of course, if things do get serious, you'll be itching to find out how he relates to your children and this could be what clinches the deal. Just remember to err on the side of caution until you're sure that the relationship has a future.

TRUE TALES....

I met this really nice guy on the Internet. We dated for about three months but I decided I didn't want to introduce him to my daughter. She already has a patchwork life: at the crèche two days a week, with her grandparents on another and at her dad's every second weekend. She didn't need another adult in her life to complicate things, unless I was serious. He also had kids from a previous marriage, so he understood my position. Unfortunately, we were just getting to the stage where we thought it was appropriate to introduce each other to the kids when he was transferred to Brisbane. It was a real shame, but I'm too practical to think we could have developed a relationship from such a distance.

Analise, 31

Do as I Say, Not as I Do

Where children are involved, morality can become a big issue, so tread carefully: even the most perfect new relationship will impact on your kids. When they're small, they can be confused by feelings of disloyalty; when they're teenagers, it can be difficult explaining why it's okay for you to sleep with someone when they can't.

That's why Kuriansky thinks that grown-up sleepovers should be reserved for very serious relationships. It may be difficult to wait, but your resolve will show your children how much you respect them, as well as demonstrating that entering into an intimate relationship is a serious decision.[2] If you need to 'sow some wild oats' it might be better to restrain yourself until the kids are on their weekend with Dad or sleeping over at grandma's. If you don't have that luxury, then get physical at your date's place while someone you trust looks after the children.

Apart from your children, you'll also have to deal with everyone else poking their nose in where it doesn't belong. Some may disapprove of your new relationship; others may make unfair judgements. As long as you're keeping your children's interests at heart, and are sensible about what you're doing, tell everyone else to get stuffed — in the nicest possible way, of course.

Be careful, though, because sometimes the advice of caring friends and family will be in your best interest. When you're head-over-heels, it's easy to overlook the signs that may indicate things are not what they seem. So, before bringing a man into your children's lives make sure you know him well. You've alerted your kids to 'stranger danger' so don't be surprised if they're wary of a newcomer in their home. Remember: in the majority of child sex abuse cases the perpetrator is someone the child knows. You'd never forgive yourself if harm came to one of your children, so never rule out the possibility that your date might not be on the level.

Happy Families

You've taken the cautious approach, reached the stage where you know and trust someone and feel ready to amalgamate your love-life with your family. Even if you've done your best to explain the new man in your life to your children, they may still resent him. 'Children will always be upset about the new love in your life no matter how much they like him,' says Kuriansky. 'Deep inside, children want their family back together. Any newcomer is bound to be perceived even subconsciously as a stranger who is sabotaging their fantasy.'[3]

To avoid a nasty surprise, make the first meeting between your children and your new man as relaxed as possible by planning fun activities, and always begin by introducing him as a friend. If you detect resentment, talk with your children about how they're feeling. You can help them express their feelings by saying things like, 'I know you feel angry with me for having a boyfriend', and then reassure them that he'll never replace their Dad or become more important than they are. If you're going to make a go of it, everyone involved will experience a period of adjustment. And most of the time you'll be the meat in the sandwich.

Support and Advice

24-Hour Help Lines

ACT Tresillian parent Help Line 1800 637 357

NSW Tresillian parent Help Line 1800 677 961

NT Phone your local health services, e.g. doctor or hospital emergency

QLD Telephone Information Support Service 1800 177 279

SA Parent Helpline 1300 346 100

TAS Parent Information Telephone Assistance Service (PITAS) 1800 808 178

VIC Parentline 13 22 89

WA Family and Children's Services 1800 654 432

Relationships Australia 1300 364 277 or 1800 817 569; www.relationships.com.au

Parent Link Click on 'parenting guides' then 'parenting on your own'; www.parentlink.act.gov.au

Family Stuff an online community for single parents; www.lm.net.au/~kmw/

Good Beginnings for advice and links to other parenting support sites; www.goodbeginnings.net.au

Solo Mums a US website for advice, support, chats, message boards, networks and links; 4mom.4anything.com/4/0,1001,4924,00.html

Parents' World a US e-zine with articles, tips, chats and links; www.parentsworld.com

World Wide Single Families a global online community; uk.internations.net/wwsfamilies

Practicalities

TIME

If your child's father is still on the scene, set aside the days that he has custody for you and your new man. If you're still on a lurve quest, forget about spring cleaning or catching up with your married friends. Instead, team up with a single friend, get out there and circulate. Depending on your mood, you can drag out the glad rags and teeter off to the nearest nightclub, or choose a cosier venue where you can mix with men and women.

The planned approach is a good idea if you've been out of circulation for a while. Introduction agencies offer a practical solution if you don't have the time or inclination to take your chances at bars and clubs. Agencies also give you the opportunity to be up-front about your family situation and the kind of man you want to meet. Of course, some are expensive, so keep an eye out for special offers. (For more tips, see Chapter 10: 'Finding ... love with paid help'.)

SUPPORT

If you have a computer with Internet access, the online world is another good method of making contact with other singles. Once the kids are tucked up in bed you can sit down with a glass of wine and use chat rooms to practice your flirting skills while you expand your social network. Some net-savvy single parents swear that they can't be bothered meeting new partners any other way. You'll also find special chat rooms and forums especially for single mums. They're a great way to make friends with people who understand your situation, as well as being a fun way to spend an otherwise boring Saturday night at home.

If you don't have Internet access at home and still want to give it a go, book a space at a public library free of charge or find one of the many Internet cafes that provide access for a small fee.

If you're wary of dating agencies or chatting to strangers, support groups like Parents Without Partners (PWP) hold social functions for singles and their ankle-biters. (Joining also gives you instant support in other towns and cities.) Your local neighbourhood centre may also be able to provide you with contacts for single parents' social groups near you. Or find a special interest club where you can learn a new skill and meet new people. Participants won't all be single, but by widening your social circle, you may just find a new friend with a lovely single brother, uncle, or dad. If that's not your bag, why not band together with other single parents and develop your own social club?

Support and Advice

Parents Without Partners (PWP)

ACT (02) 6248 6333

NSW (02) 9896 1888

QLD (07) 3275 3290

SA (08) 8359 1552

TAS (03) 6243 5007

VIC (03) 9836 3211

WA (08) 9389-8350

pwp.freeyellow.com

MONEY

If you need more childfree time, save money by organising a babysitting syndicate with other parents. Whether they're married or single, everyone appreciates a night out without having to pay babysitting costs!

If you're short of cash and can't set up a babysitting syndicate check out Chapter 9 for more ideas on 'chance' meetings. Concentrate on places that attract other single parents, like local parks, where Dads with limited custody access may be making the most of their time. Be careful of playground rage: before you start batting your eyelashes, make sure he is a *single* dad.

GREAT EXPECTATIONS

Be realistic about the type of man who will fit your lifestyle. Many men pull the plug at the first sign of commitment simply because they don't want to get involved with someone who has a family. If you keep dating these men, then maybe it's time to think about changing your pattern and reassess what you really want from a potential partner.

> **TRUE TALES....** *I met a guy who complained about how the Child Support Agency has it in for separated fathers and how his ex-wife won't let him see the kids. I then discovered that instead of agreeing on a routine, he expected his wife to give him access whenever he decided, sometimes with less than 24 hours notice. That's when I realised that single mums and dads look at parenting responsibilities from very different perspectives. As a single Mum, I knew this bloke wasn't for me.*
>
> **Felicity, 31, mother of one**

Dating Single Dads: A Package Deal

Men also can come as part of a package, although most with children don't have full-time custody. Arrangements vary from family to family, and while kids soon get their heads around the 'three-four-seven' (one example of the pattern of custody days with each parent), this new language and lifestyle might take a bit of getting used to. And you'll have to ensure that you don't take your new love interest away from his children.

Kuriansky says that when you hook up with a single parent you need to be prepared for differences in responsibilities and attitudes to avoid feeling threatened or left out.[4] In the early days, you need to go with the flow. That might mean dates are cancelled at the last minute or that he's initially reluctant to invite you into his whole life. As the relationship progresses, discuss your feelings so you both know where you stand. If strife arises between you and his kids — or your kids and his — remember that blood is always thicker than water. Green says that parents will always take sides with their children against a step-parent (or step-lover). Not because they don't care for them, are insensitive or even biased, but because a parent's natural instinct is to protect their offspring.[5] So, don't make the mistake of asking him to choose between you and his children. Invariably, you'll come off second-best.

Another stress factor that can arise when dating a man with kids is the presence of 'the ex'. All men have a history but, in most cases, his past lovers will be long gone. When children are involved, however, that's not always the case. If you're threatened by, or even jealous of his former partner, get over it! They're not together any more, so don't waste your time worrying about her. It's far more important to focus your energy on something positive, like bonding with his kids. If you do find yourself struggling, get help. There are plenty of parenting support networks (see above), or try Stepfamily Zone (www.stepfamily.asn.au) for online support, advice, clubs, resources and links.

TRUE TALES... *Mitch's daughter was a gorgeous little thing, but I couldn't stand the way he parented. As a part-time dad, he was afraid that if he disciplined her she wouldn't want to see him anymore. He felt so guilty about the relationship breakdown that he let her do whatever she wanted, including having chocolate for breakfast! He even agreed to sit on the toilet floor and read her a story while she did a poo. I was careful not to interfere, even when he sat in the back of the car with her and made me drive! We did break up, but not because of his child.*

Angela, 32

As you get older, sharing your love-life with little ones (yours or his) becomes more of a possibility. Potential minefields still abound, but when handled well these blended relationships can enrich everyone involved. Keeping a clear head and being sensitive to the needs of others is paramount. If there are too many times when you feel as if you're being torn in half, consider seeking professional help from someone who can give you objective advice and support. You might be SuperMum or SuperLover, but only those with extraordinary powers have the ability to be SuperEverything.

part 3
FINDING MEN

8. FINDING.... love in your own backyard

Dear Aunt Lurvinya,

I'm sick of my married friends trying to fix me up with a bloke! I mean, I want to find love, but do they have to be so obvious? Last week I'd arranged to meet a girlfriend for dinner. Five minutes after we sat down in walked Mr 'Oh-What-a-Coincidence-Seeing-You-Here'. I'd been looking forward to catching up on old times but my friend invited him to join us. He was actually quite nice, but their underhanded plotting hardly put me in the mood for romance. I went home early with a headache. Now I'm wondering if I should have given him more of a go. Do you think I've blown it?

Miss Matched

Dear Miss Matched,

You've blown it, all right. Not only did you let a perfectly good opportunity for potential romance slip by; you risked ruining a friendship. Your friend may have done the wrong thing, but I'm sure she did it for all the right reasons. So humour the poor misguided dear. Then apologise for being a stick in the mud, ask for Mr Coincidence's phone number and arrange to meet for a coffee. It will make her day, and he may turn out to be okay. After all, he comes with pretty good credentials. You'll no doubt have your friend

> on the phone wanting all the gory details. And since she was the one who introduced you, doesn't she deserve a few treats?
>
> *Aunt Lurvinya*

Cosy But Closed

If your social circle has narrowed — or become filled with happy-loving-couples — it can be a real stumbling block in your quest to find love. You may enjoy being with your friends, but if they're all married most won't be interested in hanging out with you in places where single men lurk. Anyway, you're less likely to be chatted up if you're with them. Of course, you may be quite cosy and rarely feel like getting 'out there' after working all week. But even in such limited environments, there are still opportunities aplenty for meeting men. The only rule is, make your feelings known. Moaning, 'I want a man, and I want him now!' will only work if someone else hears you say it. So enlist the help of colleagues and friends and put them to work. Above all, don't be afraid to admit that you're looking for lurve. As Nita Tucker says, 'asking for support is one of the best ways you can get what you want'.[1] Tread carefully though; your job and your friends are hallowed ground and once you've crossed that line it's not always easy to go back.

Finding Lurve Through Friends

THE FINE ART OF NAGGING

One of the best ways to meet men is through a friend. They come with instant recommendations, are probably not axe-murderers, and may even share common interests. So, if you really want to find love, you could do worse than thoroughly exploring this avenue. Sometimes you've got to give your friends a little push. For instance, your gal pals might not have any single male friends, but their partners might.

You've probably listened to well-intentioned friends say, 'you must meet so-and-so, you'd really get on. We'll arrange a barbecue.' Then they sit back on their contented married bums and forget all about it. Next time you're over at their place and casually ask, 'whatever happened to that single guy from Dave's work?' she'll say, 'Oh, he's madly in love. Apparently, he met a girl skiing.' 'Skiing?' you cry. 'I *love* skiing!'

To avoid such disappointment, you've got no option but to nag and nag again! If your friends are sincere, they'll get the message and make the quest to improve your love-life a priority. Of course, their idea of suitable partners may not always coincide with yours, but the chase is half the fun.

TRUE TALES...

On a weekend away with a group of friends, Bronwyn asked me what I was looking for in a man. I was actually happy being single so I just said, 'someone normal ... I'm sick of games and dickheads'.

Bronwyn said she knew a lovely man, Phil, and invited me to come along next time they went out. I agreed to join them, as long as it was casual. A foursome wasn't what I had in mind but I felt confident that she wouldn't set me up with a loser.

After we all met up, Bronwyn cornered me in the loo and said, 'Well, what do you think?' Phil got the same treatment. We both answered, 'nice'. He rang me the next day and we arranged to meet for dinner and a movie. That night, we talked so much that we never got to the movie part! Four days later, we went out again and, from that day on, we were a couple. A month later we met each other's parents, four months later we were engaged, and we were married a year to the day that Bronwyn threw us together. Of course, she was an honoured guest at the wedding.

Rosanna, 34

THE GOOD, THE BAD AND THE BORING

Remember the dinner party scene in *Bridget Jones's Diary* where Bridget sits at a table of smug married couples who can't think of anything intelligent to ask her except, 'So, Bridge, how's single life treating you?' Hopefully, your friends are more supportive and don't make you feel like a social pariah. Sometimes it can go the other way. You're looking forward to dinner with good friends and then you arrive at their place to discover you're seated next to Mr Earnest Bore. The only way you can avoid talking to him is to excuse yourself every half-hour and make a beeline for the loo. Who cares if everyone thinks you've got a bladder problem?

After your fourth visit to the powder room, Mrs Hostess sidles up behind you and whispers, 'So ... what do you think of Earnest? Nice, isn't he?'

'Hmmm,' you reply, trying to contort uncooperative lips into something resembling a smile.

'Oh goodie', she trills, waltzing you out of the room, 'I'll give him your phone number then, he just asked.'

Of course, Earnest could just as easily have turned out to be Heath Ledger's older brother. But you'd have never found that out if you'd discouraged your friend from setting you up. Unfortunately, this approach means taking the bad with the good — a delicious four-course meal punctuated by small talk from a total dud. The benefit of being set up in mixed company is that you can always chat to someone else before making your getaway. If you've been talked into a blind date, you'll have to fend for yourself. And, since the guy is a friend of friends, you'll have to be nice to him. If he turns out to be the blind date from hell, avoid bagging him to your friends. They'll feel hurt, because they only had your best interests at heart. And insulted, because you were rude enough to criticise their taste.

Blind Dates from HELL

MR SEDATIVE

Tells you all about his wallpaper sample collection, which makes him the perfect date if you've been having trouble sleeping.

MR COCKSURE

Treats the waitress with contempt, talks all night about himself, and then tries to get into your pants although you've made it clear that you don't sleep with guys on a first date.

MR OCTOPUS

You meet for a movie and dinner. Before the movie starts, he decides that he's having you for dinner.

MR APE MAN

He might be Prince Charming in disguise, but you take one look at the thick black hair on the back of his hands and poking out of his collar and decide that you aren't the woman who's going to kiss him to find out. Besides, that only works for frogs, not gorillas.

MR CREEPY

You breathe a sigh of relief when that date is over. He seemed okay at the start but as the night wore on you got the feeling that he was a bit too weird. On the way home, he took a detour to show you 'Grandma's grave'.

MR EARNEST

His smile is fixed from ear-to-ear and he agrees with everything you say. When you ask him what he's going to order, he says, 'I'll have what you're having, Babe.'

MR HEARTBREAK

He spends the entire date telling you about how much his ex-girlfriend hurt him.

MR LIMP

He lets you organise the date and choose the venue. He agrees with everything you say. When it comes to the goodnight kiss, his hands dangle loosely on your hips and he waits with lips parted for you to make contact.

If you really don't want to be matched up with Mr Surprise, be honest. Explain to your friends that, although you appreciate their efforts, you'd rather not be fixed up that way. You could suggest that if there's someone they think you'd like to meet in the future, you'd prefer a casual barbecue or drinks party. Then, if he's still a dud, at least you can escape into the crowd rather than be forced to sit next to him the entire night. Or, offer to have a party at your place and invite other singles.

Remember the days when there was always a party or three to attend on Saturday night? And remember how many men you met (and probably pashed in a dim hallway or overgrown backyard)? You may no longer be looking for a tongue rugby tournament, but throwing a party at least gets you back in the game. Ask all your friends and tell them entry is only guaranteed to those who bring along a single male friend. Encourage your friends to take a turn at being 'host'. Isn't it time you started having fun again?

TRUE TALES...

A few years ago I got together with three of my single girlfriends to arrange a cocktail party. We charged $20 a head and sold tickets to make sure we knew how many people to cater for. The only restriction we had was that everyone brought a single friend of the opposite sex. We played a few silly party games to break the ice, like passing the lifesaver along a boy-girl line on a toothpick. It was a real hoot. Everyone enjoyed themselves and we all got dates out of it. One of the girls actually met her fiancé.

Jane, 34

Finding Lurve with Male Friends

Back in the old days, people found it hard to believe that a man and a woman could be 'just friends'. Somehow, sex, even in the form of unrequited lust, always got in the way. Today, while being 'just friends' has become more acceptable between men and women, sex still seems to get in the way. In the movie *When Harry Met Sally,* what began as a 'spark' developed into a meaningful friendship. But when the line was finally crossed, their friendship was ruined, at least temporarily. The film ends with 'a happily ever after' marriage. But in real life, things don't turn out like they do in Hollywood.

TRUE TALES.... *Tim and I both did Law together at uni. We were part of a big group that used to hang around together. I never really thought of him as a potential date — in fact, both of us went out with different people from time to time. We all continued to see each other after we graduated and started working. One night I remember thinking, 'hey, Tim's not bad'. He must have thought so too, because not long after that he made a move. The whole thing was very comfortable because we didn't have to go through that 'getting to know you' stage or introduce each other to friends and family. The gang was pleased, too, except at our wedding when no one knew which side of the church to sit on.*

Kristina, 30

Crossing the line changes a friendship. No matter how hard you try to go back to the way you were, it can never be the same again. Sometimes it's not such a big issue; you can talk it through and put it in the past. If the romance leads to a meaningful love relationship, even better. After all, being friends with your long-term partner is a prerequisite for happiness. The trouble is, if crossing the line only brings about mutual regret and embarrassment, you have to ask if having sex is worth losing a best friend over.

TRUE TALES.... *Although Ben and I were just mates, there was definitely a spark. It was so easy being able to phone each other whenever we felt like it. One night the inevitable happened; we couldn't keep our hands off each other. It was great, but the games started soon after. He'd go days without even a phone call! I asked another male friend what it was all about and he told me that, to a bloke 'more than once a week' is a commitment. I wasn't interested in a commitment either, but Ben disappointed me in not being up-front about it.*

Kylie, 37

FINDING MEN

When it comes to mixing bodily fluids, flatmates fall into the same category as friends. He might well be 'there' on all the nights you're as horny hell, but he'll still be there the next morning and every morning after that. As Cox points out, sharing your flatmate's futon can make you an instant de facto. She recommends that you never sleep with a flatmate if either of you are drunk, on the rebound, horny, or need reassurance after a bad night. If feelings of love do develop between you and a flatmate, and you're certain you want to take the relationship further, remember to talk things over when you finally come up for air. The most important thing to consider when starting a relationship with someone you already live with, is to make sure to 'create space' for each another.[2] The same advice also applies when starting a love relationship with a male friend.

If you still want to do the horizontal tango, even after having come to the mutual decision that it will just be 'a temporary thing ... we both know what we're doing', keep in mind that the dynamics of your friendship *will* change. Male friends are valuable commodities, so don't risk losing a friend for the sake of a bonk! If you're after an orgasm, consider hand or battery-operated relief!

In the TV drama, *The Secret Life of Us*, flatmates Evan and Alex crossed the line, and, for a while, things looked pretty dodgy. It wasn't until the pair was faced with the realities of life — the death of a close mutual friend and an impending separation — that they managed to get their relationship back on track. In real life, there isn't a scriptwriter to conveniently whisk one of you off to New York at the first sign of trouble. So, you're going to have to do your best to cope with what life throws at you and that may mean the end of what was once a beautiful friendship. Tread carefully!

TRUE TALES....

I'd broken up with my boyfriend and was going a little mad. I'd quit smoking 18 months before that, but I was so desperate for a cigarette that I rang my next-door neighbour Craig. We hadn't spoken in years, and because I'd been infatuated with his younger brother Ben for years, I never took Craig seriously.

That night, Craig gave me cigarettes — and gin. We got along really well, but there was no 'funny business'. Instead, I realised I had a new best friend next door.

The next night I went over to see Craig again and Ben walked in. He was cool with me, even though I hadn't seen him in a year. Later, Craig and I were watching a video in his sister's bedroom with the door open (we had nothing to hide) when Ben walked past and saw us. He left a note for Craig telling him to, 'f**k her off if you want to do yourself a favour, mate!!'

I was so upset, especially since I'd always considered Ben to be the 'bee's knees'. I had no idea he didn't like me! It made me wonder if I was a bit soft on him. So I talked about it with Craig and told him why I thought Ben had written the letter (I'd always been mad about him, and I'd slept with him). It was all news to Craig.

We both laughed about how Ben had assumed we were sleeping together. The funny thing is, even though we hadn't really had urges before that, we did sleep together not long after that.

We went away together, did everything together. We were, and are, inseparable. And although we're no longer lovers, he's my best friend.

The relationship definitely changed after we'd slept together, but we're closer now. We still cuddle and give each other back rubs, which is nice. But we both know where we stand, because we talked about it.

I think it's going to be interesting if one of us meets someone we want to get involved with, because they're not going to know where THEY stand. There will probably be some readjustments, but only if a third party's involved.

Ella, 26

Finding Lurve Through Work

Many women meet their partners at work or through work connections, which is great if it all *works* out. During the flirtation stage, a budding office-romance can certainly make it a lot easier to get up in the morning: you can't wait to get out of bed, select your clothes carefully and actually arrive half-an-hour *early*. When you've just crossed the line, things can get even better: furtive glances over partitions, secret notes and email communications, even the occasional clandestine grope in the store cupboard or a snogging session in that dark pub a few suburbs away.

After a while, though, things may begin to get a little sticky: one of you gets a promotion, finds a new squeeze, admits they're married, or simply falls out of lust. And because you'll still have to maintain a professional relationship even when the thrill is well and truly gone, it pays to think very seriously before entering into such risky business. If the two of you work closely together, it gets even stickier. If he's your boss, you might want to consider a transfer to another department. If he's your married boss, you might as well hand in your resignation.

TRUE TALES...

Peter and I had begun flirting heavily at work and sending each other internal emails. One night we both stayed back after everyone else had gone home and we kissed. It was magic! Afterwards, he told me that he didn't want a girlfriend so I told him I didn't want a boyfriend, but we arranged a night out anyway.

Although we both said we didn't want a partner, I couldn't help falling in love. We had a few more hot dates before I realised Peter was serious when he'd said he didn't want a girlfriend. But since I was already totally gone, I made the mistake of telling him I loved him. He laughed! After that, going to work was heart breaking, especially when he became engaged to someone else. I didn't really get over him until he left two years later.

Naomi, 27

According to Cox, when it comes to choosing mates from work there are several degrees of 'don'ts'. She recommends that you never begin a romance with anyone who's married, in a serious relationship, your boss, 12 years younger than you and works in the mailroom (you'll lose face with your coll-eagues), or who's already 'done' the rest of the women in the office.[3] She gives the green light to romances where both parties share a similar career level or work in different departments. If true love happens with someone at the next desk, she says it's only okay if one of you agrees to move on, at least to the office next door. If you forgo this advice and launch into an intra-office affair, Cox recommends you forego 'quickies' in the stairwell, lovey-dovey emails, lovesick gazes and discussing each other's ins and outs with colleagues.

TRUE TALES...

> Mal and I taught at the same school. One year we had adjoining classrooms. We used to flirt outrageously. Before long things were starting to get serious. Thank God, the kids didn't catch us! One day we kissed in the store cupboard and never looked back. He actually left teaching the following year, so we got the space we needed. We now have three kids, a house in the 'burbs, and we're thinking about putting in a store cupboard!
>
> **Petra, 39**

A much better career move is to use the people you work with as a tool to help you find romance, rather than choose one of them as the focus of your search. As you would with your friends, tell your colleagues that you're on the lookout. Then milk their social networks for all they're worth. Even if you work in an all-female environment, there are sure to be brothers, friends, uncles, sons, mechanics … some of whom just might be single.

It's also worth joining a professional association, attending union meetings, going to industry-related seminars, workshops and functions and visiting trade shows or conventions. You'll not only increase your social circle in the process; you may even get a promotion or the offer of a better job.

Further Information

Yellow Pages Look under : 'Organisations — Business and Professional'.

Subscribe to professional and industry newsletters and journals, and search the Internet for websites related to your profession for information about seminars, events and trade shows.

Fishing for Office Romance

FINDING ... love in your own backyard   119

9. FINDING.... love further afield

Dear Aunt Lurvinya,

I'm so sick of going to pubs and bars to meet men. You can't even have an honest conversation, never mind find the man of your dreams. All you end up with is hair that smells like an ashtray. I've heard that in America there are singles' supermarkets. If you fancy someone, you put something like a roast duck in the child seat of the trolley. Do you know of any supermarkets here where I could go to meet men?

Jade Edd

Dear Miss Edd

Personally, I'd be suspicious of anyone who tried to communicate using a dead animal — especially a floppy, fatty plucked bird. It would be another matter entirely if such a supermarket were located in London's East End, where the word 'duck' could be cockney rhyming slang for something else entirely.

However, I can sympathise with your plight. Dragging out the glad rags and dragging your heels to the nearest nightclub is something most people only like doing when they can gyrate a pierced-belly with conviction. Nowadays, it's nice just to hear people talk.

Take heart, Jade. You don't need to leave your house to meet men. Just book a few free quotes for some domestic repairs. You might waste your time if the steam-cleaning man really sucks, but there could be a spark when the electrician walks in the door! If so, make sure you've got some other jobs he can do next week. Don't like the idea of deception? Then take advantage of your married friends, 99 per cent are renovating, right? So, drop in for a cuppa when tradesmen are due to call. It might turn out that your friend's plumber is just the one to unblock your pipes.

Aunt Lurvinya

Anytime, Anyplace

Many people swear that it's possible to meet a man anywhere. But if you're still hankering after that 'chance encounter', you probably won't find him at an all-female workplace, a women's only gym or a quilting class. Unless you've got licence plates that read 'RU-HRNY', you'll need to frequent places where men hang out. Not the local petrol station. But you're getting close ... on your next shopping trip, why not call into a car showroom for a browse? You don't have to buy, just walk in with a smile because you never know who you might meet 'by chance'.

Dial-a-bloke

FINDING ... love further afield

Taking a more organised approach to broaden your social life can have even more benefits. You'll not only increase your chances of meeting new people, you'll also learn a new language or discover the pleasure of Tibetan chanting. Be warned, though, this approach only works if you make yourself open and available. You can attend a thousand classes, but unless you go with a positive attitude, you might as well buy a good book. Have fun and people will be drawn to you. They may even be there looking for the same things you are.

Some people are naturally better communicators, so it's no wonder the 'chatty ones' always seem to be partnered! If you're the shy, retiring type it may help to choose activities where you'll meet people with common interests. Sharing the latest updates on a particular subject can be a good icebreaker — it may even lead to some witty repartee. Continuing education courses, art and craft workshops, team sports and organised events are great confidence builders. Even better, they give you the chance to make friendships over time, rather than trying to tell your life story to someone at a one-off event.

Just remember that wherever you decide to look for lurve, two things are essential: a pair of roaming eyes willing to make contact with members of the opposite sex and a winning smile. Men do smile back, some even stop for a chat, ask for your phone number, or suggest a drink. If you get to that stage and the feeling's not mutual, just start all over again. Be prepared for knock-backs but don't take a lack of interest to heart. Practice makes perfect!

TRUE TALES....

My married sister phoned one day to find out if I was busy. She said that the guy who'd come to install her new hot-water heater looked more like a male stripper than a plumber! Unfortunately, I was working so I couldn't get over for a perve.

A few weeks later, she was having trouble with the heater and had to call the company. She was disappointed when a different bloke turned up. He asked her who had put the heater in and she told him she couldn't remember his name. When he asked her what he looked like she said, 'gorgeous — I had him earmarked for my sister'. The next day he rang my sister to say that, 'Dave said, "Give her my number".'

FINDING MEN

I didn't want to ring a stranger but my sister was having too much fun to let it drop and found out David's email address. So, she wrote to him and eventually we made contact. We had a lovely night out which didn't end until 3a.m. Unfortunately, he seemed like a bit of a drifter and was heading off overseas so nothing eventuated. Pity. I think I would have enjoyed letting him explore my pipes!

Amanda, 39

The A-Z of Meeting Men

ADVENTURE

Anything involving an adrenaline rush — from mildly exhilarating to downright crazy — guarantees a male following. If you're looking for a life partner, however, you might want to avoid some of the more extreme sport enthusiasts, unless you're after a short-lived romance. Getting involved in adventure sports can be fun, just don't forget to bring along a supply of reliable incontinence products. If you're not up to jumping out of a plane or off a cliff, why not just watch?

Climbing mountains, abseiling down a cliff face, or jumping off while strapped to a hang-glider are all guaranteed to get your blood pumping. Rock climbing is increasing in popularity (you can even do it indoors). Then, of course, there's ballooning and skydiving to consider. To find your nearest club or venue, look in the Yellow Pages under the specific sport or try 'Adventure tours and holidays' or 'Outdoor adventure activities and supplies'. You also can just wander into your local outdoor adventure store and chat to the male sales staff about what's on offer. He may even offer to show you the ropes.

Further Information

Yellow Pages Look under 'Clubs — Ski', 'Clubs — Ballooning', 'Clubs — Bushwalking', 'Adventure Tours and Holidays', 'Outdoor Adventure

Activities and Supplies'.

Check out *Wild* the Australian wilderness adventure magazine for articles and lists of clubs and activities.

Outdoor Australia magazine also has great ideas for guided bushwalks and other tours.

Adventure Pro provides links to many other adventure sites; www.adventurepro.com.au

Climbing Australia provides lists of clubs around Australia; www.climbing.com.au

Ski.com provides information on all skiing resorts; www.skicom.au

AGRICULTURE

Rumour has it there are a lot of lonely men on the land just waiting for a good woman to take the wheel of their tractor or lend a hand with the milking. If that sounds like an offer too good to refuse, take a trip out bush and see for yourself, or ask at a dating agency. Apparently, there are many single rural men enrolled with agencies, particularly in Queensland. Even better, most are happy to drive several hundred kilometres for a date! To find out about attending a function for farmers, contact the Farmer's Federation in your state or territory, or join a discussion group or chat room on one of the many rural or farming websites.

Further Information

Yellow Pages look under 'Organisations — Primary Production & Rural' Try a keyword search for 'farmers'.

Farmwide click on 'farmwide community' for chats and events; www.farmwide.com.au

NSW Farmers click on 'what's on' for events; www.nswfarmers.org.au

Australian Dairy Farmers' Association
www.farmwide.com.au/nff/adff/adff.htm

FINDING MEN

BOATING

You don't need to own a boat to get into boating. Begin by wandering around marinas where it's the done thing to say hello to boat owners, many of whom are men. Similarly, visiting a local boat ramp on a calm day will present you with a steady stream of men launching boats. Offer to catch a rope as they approach. If you miss, don't worry, they're used to reading signals from bright red beacons.

On a windy day, head for the coast or a nearby lake to watch for sailors and wind- and kite-surfers. If you join a club, sailing can be an extremely social sport. It's a great way to meet people because there's always plenty to do while hanging around a sailing or yacht club waiting for the wind to pick up, a race to start, or to review the day's sailing over a cold beer and a snag. Start by signing up for a beginner's lesson, which typically ends with a twilight barbecue or drink. Once you've found your sea legs, you can put the word out that you're after a crewing job. Armed with a smile (and a cast-iron stomach) you'll get plenty of offers to team up and help sail other people's boats.

TRUE TALES... *I've been a member of my local sailing club for years. It's the centre of my social life. If ever I'm bored, I just head down there. There's a bar and usually someone to have a drink with. Some nights end up quite wild. I started off with windsurfing and sailing lessons, then a couple of years ago I was offered a crewing job on someone's boat and we started winning races. We entered competitions that took us travelling on the weekends. That's how I met Gary and we started going out soon after.*

Jackie, 38

If you live near a river, harbour, or lake, rowing clubs are another option. Positioning yourself by the riverbank like a damsel in distress may not be very effective, but you will be able to gauge whether or not your local club is teaming with the right sort of men. If things look promising and you fancy

FINDING ... love further afield

a bit of 'stroke, stroke, stroke' — sign up or at least join the social club.

Jet skiers may be the hoons of the waterways but speed attracts men, so chances are your water-based rev-head is male. And he probably likes high-speed and drag boats, too. There are special venues for these water sports with loads of opportunities for participants and spectators.

If you want something with little less equipment and difficulty, try canoeing or kayaking. However, these tend to be solo or pairs-sports, so you'll need to get involved in a club or take an adventure tour to meet people.

Further Information

Yellow Pages look under 'Sailing Schools', 'Clubs-Yacht', 'Clubs — Motor Boats', 'Water Skiing Centres & Resorts', 'Canoes &/or Canoeing'

Australian Canoeing Online www.canoe.org.au

Paddle Australia www.adventurepro.com.au/paddleaustralia

Rowing Australia for news and event listings; www.rowingaustralia.com.au

Australian Water Skiing Federation provides a calendar of events; www.awsf.com.au

Barefoot Australia for barefoot water skiing events; www.barefootaustralia.org.au

Australian Yachting Federation provides a calendar of events; www.yachting.org.au

CHARITY AND COMMUNITY GROUPS

Is there a better way to further your own cause than to help those less fortunate? After all, even if you don't meet anyone you like, you'll still be doing something worthwhile. Many charities organise functions and are more than happy to take your cheque for a seat at their next dinner dance or auction. You won't get to check out the guest list, so it can be a bit of a punt. But if you choose an event like the Red Cross 'Desperate and Dateless' ball, you'll have a better than even chance of hooking up with loads of like-minded 18–35-year-olds.

TRUE TALES... *I once went to a football fundraising dinner dance thinking it would be full of hunky men. There were some: two tables of football players with their girlfriends or a pained expression on their face. That left 653 seats, all occupied by pre-pubescent girls and their autograph-hunting mothers. The low point in my night was being sold a raffle ticket to win a dance with one of the players. The high point was not winning.*

Marnie, 35

Some emergency services groups hold regular functions and new faces are usually welcome. To get an invite, you'll have to know someone. So, it's time to make friends with your local copper, ambo or fireman. Going the distance can be worth the effort: the bashes are usually great fun and full of well groomed, decent blokes.

TRUE TALES... *I have been to many police functions in my time. They can vary from run-of-the-mill Christmas parties to what are charmingly known as 'Animal Nights'. (The wives don't get invited to those.) I've done OK over the years (but you'd have to be dead not to do). The trick is to go with a friend and with the attitude of having fun. It's very easy to talk to people. Most are 'decent Aussie blokes'. Generally, men out-number women by two to one. And to be honest, I don't think you'll ever find so many decent looking men in one room at the same time!*

Charlotte, 34

Further Information

Try a keyword search on the Internet under 'Functions', 'Fundraising events', or 'Charity events'

Community Aid Abroad holds regular events. To find out what's coming up in your State or Territory phone (03) 9289 9444, or visit the website and click on 'events'; www.caa.org.au/helping/index.html

The Desperate and Dateless Ball phone the Red Cross National Office on (03) 9345 1800, or visit the website; www.redcross.org.au

Phone your favourite charity and ask about upcoming events. (Look in the Yellow Pages under 'Charities & Charitable Organisations'.)

Police functions are advertised as part of a social club or an event, not as 'police balls' (which hopefully you'll get to 'handle' when you're touring the 'equipment' department). Functions happen on a regular basis, and the big squads usually throw Christmas bashes. Ask your friendly local police officer to get you a ticket.

Paramedics ask at your local ambulance station or talk to nurses in a hospital ward, who may be notified of functions.

CYCLING

A drive along any coastal road on a Sunday morning will show you how popular bike riding has become. Trouble is, the 'all-in-one-lycra-wrap-around-glasses-streamlined-helmet' look is definitely androgynous in the sitting position at least. Going by the legs can also be confusing; to eliminate wind resistance serious male enthusiasts shave or wax almost all of their body hair. Getting in the way of a couple of cyclists may be the only way to work out their sex, and you just might discover a real honey under that helmet. The rescue effort will be worth it, too, especially if you have to perform mouth-to-mouth. If in doubt, save your wolf whistling until the rider dismounts and you can check out the tackle factor.

All jokes aside, taking up cycling is a sure way to meet men but you'll need to join a club or at least some regular riders. Join the hordes that collectively take up as much room on the road as a semi-trailer and swoop into cafes like a flock of seagulls. It's a great way to spend a Sunday, and you'll get fit at the same time. (If you're brave enough to be seen in public in lycra.)

Further Information

Yellow Pages look under 'Clubs — Bicycle' and 'Adventure Tours and Holidays'.

The Hash House Harriers organise both running and biking 'hashes'. They are a real hoot; www.gthhh.com/maps/downunder.htm

Australian Cycling Federation phone (02) 9644 3002 or visit the website; www.cycling.org.au.

Specialist magazines offer articles, contacts and a calendar of events. Try *Bicycling Australia*.

Lonely Planet's *Cycling Australia* travel guide lists cycle tours.

Dancing

Partnered dancing is probably the most fun you can have with your clothes on. It's increasing in popularity and there are literally dozens of different dance styles: from salsa, jive and swing, to ceroc, tango and flamenco. (Avoid belly-dancing, however, because the only men there are the guys playing the instruments on the taped music, unless there's a 'live' drummer.) Don't worry if you have two left feet, just keep taking lessons until you get it right. It won't be long before you're throwing in a few flashy moves of your own.

TRUE TALES...

I met Anthony at a ceroc class when I was 39. We got to know each other over the months and fell in love. At our wedding, we hired a Ceroc band and did a dance number, which impressed our guests. Three years later, life together just gets better and better.
Maria, 42

Most dance styles involve a lot of direct contact with the opposite sex, but you don't have to bring a partner. During a typical session, everyone stands in rows or in a big circle — guys on one side, girls on the other — and you swap partners.

FINDING ... love further afield

At most classes, the mix of women and men is even, and many are single. Some classes are taught in licensed venues and others in a dance studio.

Further Information

Yellow Pages look under 'Dance Tuition &/or Venues' for a range of different dance styles.

Check out local gig guides for your city or town.

Ceroc Australia has venues and events around the country; www.cerocaustralia.com.au

Try a keyword search on the Internet using 'Australian Dance Links', 'Swing', 'Lebop', 'Lindy Hop', 'Latin', or any other styles you fancy.

EDUCATION

Perhaps you'd like to improve your mind? If so, enrolling in a short course or even university degree might be a good option, especially if you love learning. Try to choose a course where the gender mix will work in your favour. Like surveying, rather than quilting. To find out which courses attract more male students, phone a college or association and ask how enrolments are looking. If you're too embarrassed, ask a male friend or relative to find out how many other blokes 'do this kind of thing'.

If doing a course is part of your quest to learn how to love life, it might be just as valuable to enrol in a female-dominated course that you know you'll enjoy. Meeting new people is a way of networking and expanding your social circle. And if you let someone in the group know that you're on the prowl, they might 'fix you up'. Make good use of breaks. Cast an eye around the cafeteria and smile at anyone who looks your way.

I wanted to improve my computing skills so I enrolled in a TAFE course. A couple of times when heading along the corridor I noticed a cute looking guy in the classroom next door. One week, the student council put on free food in the caff. I found myself in the queue behind the guy from next door and my suspicions were confirmed; he was gorgeous. The girl serving must have been just as impressed because she piled so many meatballs onto his plate that there were none left for anyone else. He turned and offered to share his balls with me. What could I say! We had a laugh (and I even ate some of his balls!). The following week we had a brief chat in the break and started to sit together every week. When the end of term approached, I took a deep breath and suggested a break-up drink at the pub over the road. We've been going out ever since.

Denise, 31

Further Information

Evening classes are offered at many community centres, Councils of Adult Education, TAFE colleges, Universities and Tertiary colleges and some private organisations. (Courses that have a high male enrolment include computing, wine appreciation, finance and photography.)

FINDING ... love further afield

Yellow Pages look under 'Business Colleges', 'TAFE Colleges', 'Technical and Trades Colleges', 'Universities & Tertiary Education Colleges', 'Tuition — Educational', 'Photography &/or Video Schools', 'Cooking Classes', 'Art Schools', 'Drama Tuition', 'Language Instruction', 'Radio & Television Schools', 'Teachers — Woodworking'.

Specialty classes are often run by hotels, restaurants, wineries, and kitchen wear and gourmet food shops. These are very popular with both men and women.

The Dial is a database with listings for adult learning around Australia; www.thedial.com.au

FISHING

Catch yourself a man? Well, if you wander up and down piers it's easy to strike up a conversation with a fisherman. Just ask, 'caught anything?' If they're the silent type or are concentrating on getting a bite, you'll soon get the vibe, so move on, or ask their advice about getting yourself tackled up. They may just take your bait.

If you want to get serious, join an angling club and get involved with one of their social activities or competitions.

Further Information

Yellow Pages look under 'Clubs — Angling'.

Fishnet Australia features an online directory of local fishing clubs and associations; www.fishnet.com.au

FLYING

Most little boys dream of being able to fly. Some stick to their dream and take up flying as an adult hobby or become professional pilots. Be warned though, learning to fly is very expensive, so unless you have a burning desire to become a pilot then concentrate on being a spectator.

Air shows are good man-spotting venues, as are landing and take-off sites for hang gliders.

> ### Further Information
>
> **Yellow Pages** look under 'Clubs — Flying and Gliding', 'Hang Gliding &/or Parachuting', 'Flying Schools', 'Parachuting Instruction &/or Displays'.
>
> **Pacific Flyer** provides information on flying events and air shows; www.pacificflyer.com.au/events2.htm

GAMBLING

Take a punt and check out the talent at your nearest casino, TAB, pokie-filled pub, or the horse or dog races. Whether you fancy horses or dogs, racing happens all year round and can be good fun if you go with a friend. (You'll find the better-dressed men in the members' stands.)

> ### Further Information
>
> **Yellow Pages** look under 'Clubs — Coursing & Kennel', 'Clubs — Racing & Hunt'.
>
> **Check your weekend papers** for racing guides and details of venues.
>
> **The Australian Jockey Club** also lists events; www.ajc.org.au

GYMS

If you can get past the problem of 'the male gaze' (or the compulsion to perform for it), as well as the testosterone-laced sweat on the equipment and having to readjust the weights from 50kg to 5kg, a mixed gym offers a really great opportunity to meet men. You don't have to rely on a one-off meeting, just keep an eye out for someone interesting and move from a non-threatening smile to a hello. Not all men who go to gyms are beefcakes; some are just there to get fit and meet other people, so they can usually manage more than a grunt.

Male personal trainers are also an option (that's how Madonna got her first child!), but you may want to be sure of your trainer's motives before you give him the green light to 'read' your vital statistics.

LIFESAVING

When you were a teenager, did you park your towel near the surf lifesaving club to check out the talent? Why stop just because you're a grown-up? Not all lifesavers are 15-year-old boys, and even if they are, they might have an available dad or uncle. Instead of the old 'rescue me' approach, why not get involved with a surf lifesaving club by helping with fundraising as a worthwhile way of expanding your social circle? If you're keen, join as an associate or train to become an official or lifesaver yourself. You never know who you might rescue!

Further Information

Surf Lifesaving Australia has centres around the country:

New South Wales (02) 9984 7188

Northern Territory (08) 8941 3501

Queensland (07) 3846 8000

South Australia (08) 8356 5544

Tasmania (03) 6231 5380

Victoria (03) 9534 8201

Western Australia (08) 9244 1222

www.slsa.asn.au

MOTOR VEHICLES

Many men gravitate to anything that involves speed or engines. That often means cars. There are associations or clubs for just about every make of car, from an Alpha Romeo to a Zephyr. Unless you're planning on trading in your standard 90s hatchback for a vintage jalopy, stick to displays and auctions, where you can 'ooh' and 'ah' over the beautiful bodies. There might even be some nice cars there, too. If you want to get behind the wheel, ring around to find out about opportunities to take part in rallies. Even if you don't drive, you can still prove that women can read maps.

If full-on motor racing isn't your thing, consider an advanced training course or take up four-wheel driving. You can be a passenger in a four-wheel drive tour: vehicle owners follow as 'tagalongs' so you won't be stuck only with the people in your car.

Motorbike clubs are also male-dominated and some even have facilities for women. If gravel-rash isn't your bag but you'd still like to try something speedy, get into go-kart racing. There are venues in most cities and large towns. Why not organise a group of friends for a team race?

Or, just take your own car down to the local car wash where a team of men will cater to your every whim. Well, at least your car's whims. You never know, like Ally McBeal (who had sex with a stranger in a car wash) your car might not be the only thing that gets a good service. Many car washes now feature on-site cafes, so why not offer to buy a coffee for the nice guy polishing your windscreen? (It'll be easy to strike up a conversation, because he'll have his name sewn on his shirt!) Self-service car washes also have men-spotting potential; after all, washing the car is a thing that men generally seem to be keener at doing than women.

So go alone, ask the best looking bloke for a demonstration and milk it for all it's worth. Tell *'Bill'* that the only thing you hate about being single is having to wash your own car. You'll be giving him just the right mix of messages.

Further Information

Yellow Pages look under 'Clubs — Car', 'Adventure Tours and Holidays', 'Driving Schools', 'Go-Kart Hire' or 'Clubs — Motor Racing'.

Ask at a local tourist office for information about your nearest speedway track.

Bike Point Australia lists clubs and events for motorcycle enthusiasts; www.bikepoint.com.au

V8 Supercars Australia lists events and social activities; www.v8supercars.com.au

Misty Mountains 4WD Tours www.mistymtns42dtours.com.au

Outback Tagalong Tours www.outbacktagalong.com.au

Swagman Outback www.swagmantours.com.au

NIGHTLIFE

Although it's a dating jungle out there, meeting significant others in smoky pubs, clubs and bars does happen. It's just a matter of finding the right places. Small bars, local pubs and clubs with a narrow focus, like jazz music, are a better bet than 'meat-markets', singles' bars or nightclubs. Try out a few different venues to discover where you feel most comfortable.

Becoming a regular at a darts or pool night, or at a small pub or club can help. And once people start to recognise you, it's easier to strike up a conversation. Even if you don't fancy someone straight off, the idea is to expand your social circle. The added advantage of becoming a regular is that going alone becomes less of a problem. There will always be someone to team up with.

PETS

Walking a dog has long been seen as a great way to meet men — and watching how he relates to Fido can be a great indication of his personality — or lack of it. It's easy to strike up a conversation — especially if your dog takes a shine to his (or vice versa). You may even be able to discover what type of person he is by his breed of dog. For example, he'll either be loyal and lovable, aggressive and loud, fat and lazy, or someone who'll always be on your tail.

TRUE TALES...

I was furious after waiting in vain during my lunch break for the horse dentist to turn up. At four o'clock, the girl at the paddock rang to let me know he was on his way. I excused myself from the office and drove like a madwoman to the paddock. I didn't even have time to exchange my heels for my Blundstones. I got out of the car ready to give him a piece of my mind, but when I saw his smile it was hard to stay angry. Half an hour later I left with his business card and the feeling that I'd met someone special.

Henrietta, 38

You can also use cats, rats, guinea pigs, fish, birds anything that walks, slithers or crawls to increase your chances of meeting males of the two-legged variety. Look for clubs and shows for pet enthusiasts. If you are into horses (recommended only for those with a lot of time and money on their hands), keep your eyes open for single farriers, vets, horse dentists and trainers. Or visit Quarter Horse events, which tend to be more male-dominated than other horsey activities.

Further Information

Yellow Pages look under 'Clubs — Bird' (from canary clubs to homing pigeons), 'Clubs — Dog', 'Clubs — Pet', 'Dog training', or 'Horse Riding'.

Your local Animal Welfare League or RSPCA may also hold events for you and your pet.

FINDING ... love further afield

PLACES OF WORSHIP

Don't dismiss churches or synagogues as outdated venues for meeting potential partners. If you hold a particular set of values or beliefs, it's likely that you're looking for someone with similar views. This doesn't mean that you're going to lock eyes with a hunky new minister during next Sunday's service. But joining a church group with people of your own age group will expand your social circle.

POLITICS

Why do people give up great chunks of their time to become politicians? Is it the lure of power, the thought of kissing babies, passionate views, a desire to contribute to society, or simply something to get them out of the house? Perhaps it is an easy avenue for a born liar to realise their potential. So, if you do meet someone through politics and give him your vote of confidence, be prepared. He might just go back on his promise to love, honour and cherish.

If you are sure about your own political standing, then becoming involved with a political party is a sure way to expand your social circle. Membership involves helping in the office, campaigning, making phone calls, contributing to newsletters, organising or attending fundraisers, attending meetings and/or running for public office. Each major party has a local branch network, or you could try your luck on the local council. You never know where it might lead, handing out voting cards one day, Prime Minister the next.

Further Information

Yellow Pages look under 'Organisations — Local Government', 'Organisations — Political'.

Parliament of Australia, Parliamentary Library contains a complete listing of political parties registered with the Australian Electoral Commission. There are links to their individual websites where you'll find info on joining or volunteering; www.aph.gov.au

RODEOS

If you like 'real men' in denim and boots, rodeos might be the place for you. Forget trying to catch a cowboy's eye in the stocks, he'll be too busy psyching himself up to tackle that bucking bull or bronco. A better option is to hang around the bar and offer to buy Mr Handsome a beer. Sometimes the drinking can continue 'til the wee hours and move to an after venue.

TRUE TALES...

I've got a bit of a thing for cowboys. I have a horse myself so I've always really enjoyed rodeos, but it's afterwards that the real fun begins. In my opinion, every woman should do herself a favour and 'have' at least one in her lifetime. I've had three. One broke my heart but you know what they say — if you fall off, you've just got to get right back on and keep riding!

Mel, 39

Be warned: cowboys live a roving life and settling down might not be a high priority. A good time every time he's in town is more the ticket, so beware the sensitive heart! You might be better off keeping your eyes peeled for other spectators. Dress tips: if you want to be noticed, wear a skirt; if you want to blend in, get yourself a pair of Blue Dog or Wrangler jeans. Either way, mudproof shoes are essential.

Further Information

Australian Bushman's Campdraft & Rodeo Association lists a 'what's on' page; www.abcra.com.au

Australian Professional Rodeo Association lists upcoming events on their website; www.prorodeo.asn.au

Running

Visit any popular running track any day of the week (be early) and you'll be rewarded with a steady stream of power-walking, jogging or running men. Smile as they pass by, and be there the following week. Once you get the hang of it, you may even be able to catch up and have a chat. Trouble is, you'll probably feel more like chucking than talking. This is because, when running, the average decent looking bloke transforms into something resembling a slimy extraterrestrial: hair plastered to his face, wobbly bits jiggling up and down, clothes smelly and wet, veins bulging from his neck and sweat streaming from every pore. Try to avoid thinking of how much he might sweat in bed.

If you become a runner yourself, you'll be able to empathise. You'll feel hot, but (apart from the rosy cheeks) you might not look it. You will, however, get fit *and* vastly improve your chances of meeting men, especially if you take part in marathons, fun runs or join a running club. All have a high rate of male participation and some, like the Hash House Harriers, combine fitness with social events.

Further Information

The Hash House Harriers is a worldwide running (and drinking!) club with a number of branches in Australia. Look in your local Yellow Pages under 'Clubs — Sporting Miscellaneous', or visit their website to find a club near you; www.gthhh.com/maps/downunder.htm

Runner's World magazine lists runs around Australia and advertises upcoming events. Once you register for an event, you'll receive info on others; www.ausrun.com.au

Triathlon Australia lists events that combine running, cycling and swimming; www.triathlon.org.au

SCUBA DIVING AND SNORKELLING

Combine technology with adrenaline-laced adventure and it's no wonder that scuba diving is a popular sport amongst men. You'll need a keen interest to become involved, as it can be expensive, and requires a well-developed sense of adventure and water confidence. If that sounds like you, stop putting it off and get out there. (Or, should I say, *under* there — especially if you're into rubber.) Snorkelling doesn't require as much equipment and there are clubs and schools at many local beaches. The world will never look the same again after you've seen what's under the waves.

Further Information

Yellow Pages look under 'Scuba Diving Schools', 'Clubs — Scuba Diving', 'Divers — Recreational'.

Diving in Australia has information about clubs and events around Australia, as well as links to other sites and a page to help you find a dive buddy; www.divingaustralia.com.au

Check out one of the many diving travel guides in any good bookshop.

SHOPPING

To track down male shoppers, just think fast and loud; everything motorised, electrical or outdoorsy; and anything gadgety aimed at Mr Fix-its. Men run their fingers along the shiny hub of a motorbike like we do a silk bedspread, they examine a Swiss army knife the way we investigate the workings of a pump-up bra. Try not to be too obvious, just bring along a list of questions for sales staff and don't be afraid to ask them, or other shoppers, for advice.

If you're looking for someone like Tim 'the Toolman' Taylor (or even his sidekick, Al), a hardware store is your best bet. But stay away from those suburban hardware barns on weekends to avoid being the only single in a sea of renovating couples. Your best bet is a city store at lunchtime, or a specialty trade store for electrical or plumbing supplies.

Hi-fi and music stores are also filled with a largely male clientele, as are surf shops. But some women swear that supermarkets are the best place to find single men: check the contents of their trolley and steer clear of men who've loaded theirs with tampons and nappies. Shopping late in the evening at inner city or suburban fringe supermarkets is your best bet.

SPECIAL INTEREST GROUPS

If you want to meet people who share your drives and passions consider joining a special interest group or social club. You'll find everything from stamp collectors to dowsing societies. Social clubs based on ethnicity are also a good way to meet people of a similar cultural background. Start by browsing through the 'clubs' listings in your local Yellow Pages. If anything grabs your attention simply phone and ask if you can attend a function as a guest to find out about the members before you sign up. If you think you'll fit in, and want to raise your profile, join a committee or offer to help with administration.

If you're stuck for ideas, think about joining a chess club. It's a great place to learn 'all the right moves' and perhaps meet a white knight. You also could try photography. Put yourself 'in the picture' by learning a new skill as well as meeting some snappy guys. Film appreciation groups are an inexpensive way to see movies and discuss them with other aficionados. Although gem and lapidary clubs may sound a bit down to earth, you may just find a diamond in the rough. For something a little more cultural (highbrow or popular), you could expand your interest in music by joining light opera or instrumental groups, music societies, fan clubs or a vinyl collectors club.

For *Red Dwarf* or *Star Trek* fans and believers of UFOs, the truth is out there: you'll find a range of interest groups where you can talk about or create heavenly experiences of your own. Joining a computer club and attending computer expos and swap meets are surefire ways of meeting men. But, if you don't speak the lingo, you might need to take an interpreter. Then again, you could just ask the best looking cyborg to show you his hard drive.

Further Information

Yellow Pages look under 'Clubs' (listed individually) or 'Clubs — Social & General', 'Societies — General' (includes guilds, friendly societies and music societies).

Check out local newspapers under columns headed 'seeking a friend', 'social group', 'sports and activities', or the 'what's on' section.

Try keyword searches on the Internet to find loads of other specialised groups or key in 'club' for more ideas.

SURFING

Not all surfers are teenagers. In fact, you'll find plenty of former-teenagers riding surfing's new waves. And, since the development of the modern Malibu (easier to ride than a shortboard), older men are coming to the sport for the first time. Head for surfing meccas like Victoria's Phillip Island (aka 'bloke island') and Torquay, Queensland's Noosa Heads or Gold Coast, Byron Bay and Newcastle in NSW, and WA's Margaret River region for your next holiday.

Surfing lessons and clinics for women and girls are also becoming popular, so why not paddle out and give it a go. But beware: don't hang around with the big boys until you wise up on your surfing etiquette. Dropping in on someone else's wave is not only bad karma it can be downright dangerous. Practice on baby waves close to shore, then loiter with your board (à la Gidget) to see if your Moondoggy emerges from the surf. After dark or when the surf isn't 'up', try beachside bars, cafes and pubs where you'll find hordes of men opting out of the mainstream for mid-life soul and surf-searching quests.

> ### Further Information
>
> **Surfing Australia** lists clubs and events; www.surfingaustralia.com.au
>
> **Ask about events** at your nearest travel agent or at 'serious' surf shops (*not* surf fashion outlets).
>
> **Check out surf travel guides in any good bookshop.**

SWIMMING

Many men like to get in a few laps before or after work and at lunchtime. Why not investigate one of the larger city swimming pools and aquatic centres where you can join squads or clubs and combine swimming lessons with social activities. After all, a pool is the perfect place to get a preview of 'the package' (especially if he's wearing Speedos — aka 'budgie smugglers'). An added advantage of seeing him undressed is that it rules out nasty little surprises like the 'hairy back', or at least gives you time to get used to it. So take the plunge and get fit while you're at it.

> ### Further Information
>
> **Yellow Pages** look under 'Clubs — Swimming', 'Swimming Schools &/or Coaches'.
>
> **Try a keyword search** on the Internet under 'swimming', 'swimming lessons' or 'swimming clubs'

TEAM SPORTS

This very broad area is definitely worth pursuing. Remember, apart from beer, there's nothing an Aussie bloke loves more than joining with some other blokes (and the odd sheila) to run around an oval. You don't have to be very coordinated because most social clubs are just an excuse to get together — the ball is just an accessory. If you're a bit of a klutz, try joining a club or taking lessons. If you're not too keen on getting tackled, choose something like touch footie or become an ace spectator.

You'll also find local teams playing basketball, squash, volleyball, archery, baseball and softball, lawn and ten-pin bowling, billiards and snooker, fencing, golf, hockey, lacrosse and tennis. You could even investigate a fringe sport like Gaelic hurling. (Not what you think, and the accents are adorable.) And, remember: sign up for a *mixed* team!

Further Information

Yellow Pages look under 'Indoor Sports', 'Organisations — Sporting', 'Sports Training Services', or 'Clubs' (where popular sports are listed individually). Some of the lesser-known sports are listed under 'Clubs — Sporting' and 'Clubs — Social & General', while 'Clubs — Miscellaneous' lists everything from angling to yachting. You can also try 'Sports Tours and Holidays' and 'Sport Centres &/or Grounds'.

SportNet click on 'find a club' for a massive listing of sports clubs around Australia; www.sportnet.com.au

TRADE SHOWS

You'll find people at every stand only too eager to chat (well, they are there to sell you something). If you visit later on in the exhibition, their enthusiasm for 'the spiel' may be beginning to waver, so target good-looking male stand holders with your witty conversation and watch their eyes light up. To improve your men-meeting opportunities, choose fairs that will have a high male interest, like motor and boat shows. However, even cooking and craft shows have a good sprinkling of males (but most of them are exhibitors rather than visitors).

> ## Further Information
>
> **Yellow Pages** look under 'Exhibitions', then phone your nearest exhibition centre for information on upcoming events.

TRAVEL

Travel is one of the best ways to meet new people and broaden your horizons. People tend to make friendships more easily in unusual, exotic or arduous environments. Join a group tour, or look into one of many holiday packages and resorts designed specifically for singles. Avoid intimate romantic getaways and B&Bs, unless you're keen on spending your time gazing at loads of happy, loving couples. You'll find plenty of ideas from your local travel agent or one of the many travel websites itching to get your business.

A word of warning: holiday romances can be passionate, thrilling affairs but they can end in tears. Distance isn't the only stumbling block; it also can be difficult getting to know someone when you're in unfamiliar territory. If you project your fantasies onto a seemingly ideal man, you might discover he's not the lover you thought he was once you get him on home turf.

That's not to deny that many long-term partnerships have sprung from holiday romances. But longevity is usually the result of patience and an ability to keep a clear head. If you do meet someone who lives on the other side of the state or the globe, make sure you spend time in each other's home before making the big move or allowing him to do the same.

TRUE TALES...

I met Freddie in Zanzibar when I went on a 'spice tour' he was leading. He was really nice and asked me out, but I declined (safety first!). He begged me to reconsider, so I agreed to meet him in a public place. I was very reserved at first but things got romantic quite quickly. He was really sweet.

I continued travelling, but we stayed in touch. When Freddie asked me to come back I thought, 'what the hell' and took a big risk by returning to Zanzibar. We spent a few weeks together and I went home with a big dose of love and malaria!

We continued our long-distance romance and Freddie eventually decided to come to Tasmania. We had three months to make up our minds about each other, because we had to get married for him to get a visa. I was nervous, but it all worked out. We've just had our first baby: a lovely little coffee-coloured boy.

Martha, 35

You don't have to leave the country to travel: just become a tourist in your own town. Start at the local tourist office where you can pick up some maps and brochures and follow the tourist trail. You may just run into a tall, dark and handsome Latin Lover who'd be delighted to meet an experienced tour guide. But remember: meeting travellers is likely only to produce a 'holiday romance' — unless, of course, you're prepared to move to Barcelona.

Volunteering

Volunteering is a great way to meet new people. Choosing a cause that you really care about gives you the opportunity to meet people with a similar outlook on life, as well as being extremely rewarding. There are many organisations that would welcome your help, from Amnesty International, Greenpeace and Community Aid Abroad, to local welfare organisations and city missions.

If you're an animal lover, contact your local RSPCA or animal welfare organisation. Many community service organisations, such as Rotary and Lions Clubs, combine social functions with charitable activities. Or, why not sign up to serve on a committee in your local school, church, or community centre?

If you think you have what it takes to train for a skill-based service group, contact the St John Ambulance Association, the Country Fire Association, or a ski patrol. Or volunteer your services at a one-off event like a National Heart Foundation barbeque or a sporting event.

You don't need to sign up for life, just start with a small commitment, maybe one evening a month. And remember, investing your time and energy for others is an investment in your own sense of self-worth and spirit. No contribution is too trivial.

Further Information

Yellow Pages look under 'Clubs — Community Service', 'Organisations — Church and Religious', 'Organisations — Disadvantaged Groups Aid', 'Charities & Charitable Organisations', 'Organisations — Civil Rights', 'Organisations — Conservation & Environmental'.

Seek Volunteer is a database where you'll find thousands of vacancies to choose from once you've keyed in the organisation, your location, the work you fancy and how much time you can devote; www.volunteer.com.au

Australian Volunteer Search works like Seek Volunteer, above; www.volunteersearch.gov.au

WINE

Learning the ins and outs of fine wine is becoming an increasingly popular — not to mention enjoyable — way to socialise. Events include everything from intimate tastings and dinners to specialist events and wine shows. If you've got a good nose (or at least a penchant for spouting bullshit), and don't mind red teeth, you could find yourself in paradise. Be warned though, real enthusiasts are spitters not swallowers; start slurring your wordsh and you'll rishk being shpotted ashz a phoney (or at least a lush).

TRUE TALES...

I did two wine appreciation courses with a friend and we ended up making friends with loads of people in the business. We also became great friends with the guy who ran the course (also a wine rep). He often invites us to special tasting evenings arranged by his company for their wineries as a marketing exercise. My friend is now doing a wine science course at Charles Sturt University and does vintage at a few NSW wineries. She sometimes invites me along to seminars that involve dinner and a tasting.

Tina, 38

Further Information

Yellow Pages look under 'Clubs — Beer & Wine Makers', 'Clubs — Social & General', and 'Wine Guilds and Societies'.

Check out major and local newspapers, wine magazines and gourmet guides for events and courses.

Australian Wine Online has information on wine shows, organisations and tours; www.winetitles.com/awol

The Wine Society features a diary page; www.winesociety.com.au

WOOD

If you're keen on meeting the type of handsome woodsman who saved Snow White's life by lying to the Wicked Queen, you could do worse than visit woodworking galleries and exhibitions. They're full of talented men who like demonstrating what they can do with a log or two. Who knows, you may end up with a new suite of solid wood furniture made from reclaimed timber by a funky young artisan — à la Carrie Bradshaw.

> ## Further Information
>
> **Woodlink** has a 'what's on' list; www.vicnet.net.au/~woodlink
>
> *Australian Wood Review* magazine has a 'wood diary' page.

ZOOS

Go ahead and laugh, but it's hard to round off an A–Z guide without a 'z'! Anyway, a visit to a zoo or wildlife sanctuary isn't such a bad idea. As well as the usual array of cute furry creatures, zoos can be a great place to meet up with weekend 'custody Dads', zookeepers and tourists. All possibly worthy recipients of a little 'monkey business'.

And So ...

The world really is full of men (well, at least half full). You just need to know where, when and how to look, and always keep your mind and your eyes wide open. Before you know it, you'll be wondering how you can settle for just one. Happy hunting.

10. FINDING.... love with paid help

Dear Aunt Lurvinya,

I find it hard to meet men, so I was thinking of trying a dating agency. I've heard plenty of horror stories and I don't want to have my pockets fleeced and still end up on my own. The other thing that worries me is telling my friends. I mean, imagine if I did meet someone and settle down, how could I tell people where we met! What do you think?

A. Shamed

Dear Ms Shamed,

If you hired a consultant to help you find a suitable car, people would say, 'isn't she sensible'. So why do you imagine that if you hire a consultant to help you find a suitable partner, everyone will say, 'what a desperate old tart'? If they do, tell them to get stuffed, or tell them nothing at all. Why shouldn't you take the planned approach to finding a fellow? You've made it past the first stumbling block in admitting that you're looking for love and you need help finding it. And, if you can pay your own way in the world, why can't you pay to find love?

The reality is, most people would rather hand over money to a psychic than a matchmaker. Okay, okay, so some get it right, but if *you're gonna hand over your hard earned cash, wouldn't it be better to cut to the chase?*

And shopping for a man can be great fun! Mind you there are plenty of rogues out there desperate to line their own pockets, so be selective. Explore your options and ask loads of questions. Above all, don't hand over any money until you're satisfied that the service provider can come through with the goods. Good Luck!

Aunt Lurvinya

Desperate and Dateless

Dating agencies can take the drudgery out of finding a mate. You'll probably avoid silly chat-up lines, and be able to dispense with outmoded flirting tactics. After all, once you've paid your money it's someone else's job to hand you a bloke on a silver platter — you just have to decide if he's the one for you. What could be more perfect?

So, why do so many people still believe that enlisting a professional in the quest for love is an act of desperation? Jordan Kelly, author of *The Great Australian Soulmate Search*, says too many of us are looking for love in all the wrong places, which is why a pro-active partner search makes sense in today's social climate.[1] After all, why suffer fools, or the pub circuit, if you can let someone else do your legwork.

Perhaps the stigma attached to actively seeking love has something to do with what Sills calls letting 'our dream of love become a symptom of weakness'.[2] But if we're brave enough to admit that we want love, doesn't it make sense to be willing to try all available avenues without shame? Few of us have the time or inclination to sift the wheat from the chaff, not all of us are sparkling, flirtatious conversationalists who get asked out more often than we change our undies. Some of us need a third party to get to the first date.

Introduction agencies aren't the only option. There are also organisations happy to 'set you up' for a price, or throw you together with a bunch of other singles looking for love.

Because some of these options are better value than others, you'll save money if you look for special offers before you sign on the dotted line. Do your homework and don't expect to find Mr Right on your first attempt. Look at it like shoe shopping; you may need to try on several pairs before you find one that fits.

If you decide to give the planned approach a go, remember to smile, relax and have fun. Above all, avoid giving him the 'third degree' before the entrée. Just think of it as a regular date and keep the 'getting to know you' process as natural as possible.

Singles Columns

Free, local papers are the best source for singles columns. Check out the classifieds under headings like 'Talking Friends', 'Friend to Friend' or 'Meeting Point'.

In most columns, the 'men seeking women' ads easily outnumber those from 'women seeking men'. So, if you're not so keen on placing an ad yourself, try to entice one of the many men eagerly waiting for your reply. It's a bit of a lottery, because all you get are a few lines to make your decision from. But here are some clues to help you see through the myths.

Watch out for very brief messages like, *'Call me if u want 2B happy'*. Most papers offer the first dozen or so words free, which doesn't leave much room for more apt descriptions, like cheapskate. You could end up like Rose in Melbourne, whose date thought he'd win her love by taking her to the Myer Bargain Basement and buying her a large bucket of chips from the food court.

Abbreviations fall into the same category as impressive one-liners. Like this one: *'Guy, 34 emp n/s GSOH GL DTE s/d SNAG'*. It may seem like he's looking for an alien, but what he's really saying is: he's an employed, non-smoker, with a good sense of humour, good-looking, down-to-earth, a social drinker and a sensitive new-age guy. Watch for cute little 'logos'; they cost more, so he may be serious. You'll get a good idea of his intentions if the logo is a cutsie heart on a pair of legs!

A better bet could be a message headed with a large set of lips that says, *'Great Kisser'*. Sounds promising, and if it continues with *'Intelligent, spiritual with nice teeth and a six pack'*, he may even be ready to start a long-term relationship. Possibly worth a phone call, even if the six pack turns out to be something stuck to the ice at the bottom of his fridge. If you see a message that's over the word limit (costs more), headed with capital letters and includes, *'Not from the usual mould,'* you can assume he's tired of the singles' scene. (But the usual mould could mean something fungal.)

TRUE TALES... *I was looking through the local paper for a photographer for my wedding when my eyes wandered to the singles columns on the same page. I saw an ad that read 'BUSY 38yo dark, handsome business man seeks girl 25–35 for casual fun'. I couldn't help wondering if I should have one last fling.*

Then I spotted 'Single Dad 33yo 6ft blond and blue eyes, athletic body seeks 25–33 yo lady who knows what she wants'. I thought, gee, he sounds nice. Maybe he's a lonely widower with blond, blue eyed kids? I was daydreaming about being single and thinking about how much he would like a nice girl like me when I thought, 'Hang on, I'm getting married in a few months!' Still, it's fun to look, isn't it?

Martine, 24

The only way to find out what Mr Classified is really like is to take the plunge and ring the number. It's a simple process: you phone in to access individual voice mailboxes for a charge of around $2.20 a minute. Sometimes the person who's placed the ad will leave a pre-recorded message, so you can hear his voice before deciding to leave a reply. He can also listen to replies and respond to any messages he likes the sound of. Remember: the best ads get the most responses, so don't be disappointed if he doesn't phone back, he may have been inundated.

To protect your privacy, it's a good idea not to give out personal details until you know who you're talking to. Leave a mobile number rather than your home number, or think about getting a mobile strictly for dating purposes. Another option is to place your own ad, which gives you a bit more control over the process. At the very least, you can hear his voice before deciding to ring back.

Safety First!

Never give out your home address.

Never meet at his home or yours.

Always meet in a busy, public place, familiar to you, and always let a friend know when and where you are meeting.

If you're nervous, plant a 'spy' who can rescue you after you give a pre-arranged signal.

Start with a drink or coffee rather than dinner; it could be torturous if it's a case of instant repulsion.

The problem with placing your own ad is getting over any humility you may have. After all, you're going to have to describe your many charms and accomplishments. In this case, less is more: a short, eye-catching message may be all it takes to attract the right guy. It depends on what you're looking for, but it's probably wise to avoid something like *'herpes female seeking relationship'*. Of course, you may want to gild the lily, but don't spin too many little white lies and make sure you define the type of relationship you're after.

The fun starts once you've placed your ad and you can start checking your messages. This can cost anything from 50c to $2.20 a minute. If you like how the respondents sound, it's up to you to call them back. Start with a chat and if you get good vibes, progress to a meeting in a public place (where you can make a fast get-away if he doesn't live up to expectations).

True Tales...

I answered a personal ad in the paper and the guy called me back. He was a teacher and sounded really nice. The next week at my favourite bar, I started talking to a cute guy I'd met there before. He started telling me about his teaching job and the penny dropped! I asked him if he was the guy from the ad and he turned a bright shade of red. Unfortunately, I never saw him again.

Luisa, 29

Singles Parties and Social Clubs

TRUE TALES... *I've been to singles functions and had an absolute ball. If you go with the attitude of having fun, you usually do! I've met heaps of men and women, and some have become good friends. It's more like networking than 'picking up', although you can pick up if you want to. I certainly got asked out a lot, and dated a few guys. I didn't meet my long-term partner but I had a lot of fun.*

Brenda, 38

Attending singles' functions can be just as daunting as hanging around a city bar on a Friday night, but at least you all know why you're there. Ring around to find out if you can go along for a peek before committing to anything regular. As they say, 'nothing ventured nothing gained'.

Further Information

Australia-wide

Yellow Pages look under 'Introduction Services — Social' for organisations that run events rather than matchmaking services.

The classified sections of your local paper, and the gig guides of the weekend newspapers, may list upcoming singles' events.

Events4Singles lists events in most major cities around Australia; www.events4singles.com

SinglesEvents also has lists of events; www.singlesevents.com.au

Sydney

Chart runs dance parties each Saturday night for 28–45s; (02) 9417 6670

Robin's Singles House Parties (02) 9976 3051

Julianna & Friends theatre nights, dinners, cocktail parties; (02) 9960 5115, www.juliannaandfriends.com.au

Cloud 9 dance parties (02) 9820 6722

Melbourne

Youngs Social Club is a social group for both married and single people (not a singles club per se). Hosts regular functions, including formal black tie events; (03) 9872 5799, www.youngs-promotions.com.au

Clique Rendezvous small cocktail parties and events; (03) 9534 0117

Match Mates House Party for 30 to 50 people at a time; (03) 9563 6999

Gina's Place house parties on Saturday nights in Vermont; (03) 9872 5388

Phoenix Lifestyle Club functions for single professionals; (03) 9886 9994

Adelaide

The Café Club dinners, parties, movies, picnics; (08) 8322 9083 or (08) 8277 7967, www.picknowl.com.au/homepages/singles/cafe.htm

Brisbane

Executive Singles Social Group cocktail parties, dinners and events; (07) 3321 5858

The Social Calendar of Brisbane dinners, breakfasts, Friday night cocktail evenings, monthly dance parties, bbqs; (07) 3358 6172, www.thesocialcalendarofbrisbane.com/index.htm

The Singles Club dance parties, bushwalking, cruises; (07) 3269 9945

Tasmania

Quality Dining Company dinner, cocktail and theme parties; (03) 6224 1877

Perth

The Cowan Club various functions; (08) 9228 9223

Singles Activities and Travel

Joining a club or activity group specifically for singles can take the pressure off meeting new people. If you're shy, striking up a conversation can be easier when you have a shared interest. If you feel uncomfortable wearing a 'singles' badge, try a course. You increase your chances of meeting like-minded people and have a common focus (other than the fact you are all single).

TRUE TALES... *I was touring solo around Kangaroo Island and one evening I arrived late at the motel dining room. Ten pairs of eyes turned to stare when I sat down with my book. People looked at me and whispered, and I felt embarrassed when a couple invited me to join them for dessert. I was quite comfortable being alone, but my presence seemed to put the other diners on edge. I decided that next time I'd either have dinner in my room or travel with a group.*

Lily, 27

Travelling with other singles also makes sense. It means you can avoid being the only single parent at a family resort, or the only solo on a bus tour, which can really take the shine off a relaxing holiday.

Further Information

Singles Travel Connections organise group tours specifically for singles or will help you find a companion for independent travel; (08) 8293 6988, www.singlestravel.com.au

Chris Kaine & Associates Pty Ltd run a service that puts like-minded people in touch with one another. You fill out a questionnaire and nominate your current leisure interests and the new activities you'd like to try. It costs $50 to DIY (using an online interactive database) or $150 to let them find you a match; www.peoplebrokers.com.au

Melbourne

Phoenix Lifestyle Social Club features a 'learning annexe' with courses and seminars; (03) 9886 9994

Sydney

Julianna and Friends organises tennis rallies, barbeques, bushwalking, movie nights, parasailing and more; (02) 9960 5115, www.juliannaandfriends.com.au

Brisbane

The Social Calendar of Brisbane offers sports, movie nights, wine tastings and more; (07) 3358 6172, www.thesocialcalendarofbrisbane.com/index.htm

Mikart is aimed at singles 25-50 years old, interested in various outings, activities and walks; (07) 3395 3311

The Singles Club holds dances, parties, bushwalks and cruises; (07) 3269 9945

Adelaide

The Café Club promotes movies and festivals; (08) 8322 9083 or (08) 8277 7967

Just Good Friends is a social group for professional singles aged 28 and over; (08) 8373 4141

Perth

Jan Cowan's Introductions runs a buddy system to help you team up with other singles for a variety of activities; (08) 9228 9221, www.jcowan.com.au

Gemini Introductions runs workshops and a personal introduction service, (08) 9277 6527

Dinner Clubs

Dinner clubs for singles are another popular way to socialise. The process begins when you fill out a profile, which organisers use as a tool to bring together groups of six to eight people (always an equal number of men and women). Dinner is usually held at a local restaurant, where an agency representative will greet participants and introduce everyone, then explain how the bill is organised before departing so that the group can get to know each other. Other patrons will simply assume your group is a bunch of friends having dinner together — if they pay any attention at all.

TRUE TALES...

I have been to one 'dinner club' so far. It was something different and instead of thinking I'd never do it again, I enjoyed myself.

It was uncomfortable at first, but it didn't take long before everyone relaxed and had a great night.

It's a good way to meet people: all you have to do is make one phone call and your night is organised. There's a fair chance that you'll get along with at least one of the people at the table. I didn't actually see anyone again, but I had a good night.

Mark, 30

A one-off membership fee entitles you to as many dinners as you wish, along with the booking fee and the cost of your meal. Depending on how often you go out, this can be quite expensive. But if you enjoy wining and dining, it's a great way to kill two birds with one stone. The success of the night really depends on the mix of diners. Keep in mind that even if a particular dining agency has a very efficient compatibility profiling system, the actual chemistry between people will be what makes or breaks it, and that's something that can't be organised by anyone.

Further Information

Yellow Pages look under 'Introduction Services — Social'

Check your local paper in the 'Social Scene' or 'What's On' column for dinner clubs near you.

VIC

Dinner at Eight (03) 9699 2000

Meet At Dinner (03) 9882 6414

NSW

Match Mates (02) 9746 3231

Round Table Six (02) 9729 0230

SA

Dinner For Six (08) 8177 1766

Dinner Dating (08) 8239 0404

WA

Guess Who's Coming To Dinner (08) 9479 3814

The Dinner Club (08) 9330 8320

Dinner For Six (08) 9242 2248

TAS

Quality Dining Company (03) 6224 1877

QLD

Dinner For Six (07) 3229 6181

NT

Dinner For Six (08) 8941 7000

Dinner Connections (08) 8981 4895

Introduction Agencies

Finding love by enlisting the aid of a professional matchmaker or introduction agency is the most structured planned approach. If the service is reputable and efficient, the minute you agree to a contract your chance of meeting a man is not left to chance at all. If getting to the dating stage is your main stumbling block, then maybe you should consider this as a sensible option. Weigh the fees up against the money you might spend going from pub to bar to club in search of that enigmatic stranger. Maybe the fees aren't that unreasonable when you know that you're guaranteed a date.

TRUE TALES....

I was really nervous about using a dating agency but I saw a special offer in the paper and thought 'what the hell'. They were really nice so I calmed down and filled out the paperwork, which took about half an hour. When 'D-day' came, I was even more nervous. The guy they teamed me up with seemed nervous too, so conversation took a little while to get going. Even though he was quite sweet, he was a few years younger than I was, so I wondered if the agency had taken note of anything I'd said. The next match was really boring and then tried to stick his tongue down my neck. I was beginning to think I'd made a huge mistake when I was set up with Maurice. He was quite a bit older and very reserved at first, but I really enjoyed our conversation so we arranged to see each other again. Six months later we're still dating.

Elidia, 37

If the agency is doing their job properly, they will try to match you with someone suitable. Compatibility is usually gauged through lengthy personality profiling. You also get a say in the type of man you are looking for. Doubts remain as to the usefulness of this sort of scientific and computerised profile matching. Chemistry is something that only happens when you actually meet, it can't be predicted. Look what happened in *The Secret Life of Us* when Kelly worked in a dating agency. She sent one fellow on loads of dates with women who had high compatibility ratings on paper. In real life, they all *liked* him but there was no spark.

Protecting your Pockets

Make preliminary phone calls to find out how the agency works and how much the service costs.

Ask to see a contract and read it carefully before signing or handing over any money.

Your local consumer affairs bureau may be able to give you specific information on agencies that have won awards or received complaints.

Look out for specials — you can get quite a cheap deal if an agency is over-subscribed by men.

Pines explains that the best partnerships are when two people are 'similar in general ways ... but who complement one another in a particular opposing dimension'.[3] Differences are more exciting than similarities and we feel we are more likely to learn something new and valuable when with people who are in some ways different to ourselves. In this sense, perhaps two people can be too compatible.

If the testimonials are anything to go by, some agencies must be doing something right. As far as getting serious about finding love goes, it's a popular option. Apparently, Australian dating agencies were inundated with requests following the 9/11 attacks on the US.[4] With emotions running high, people began assessing their lives and some decided they couldn't put off finding love and cut to the chase.

> **Further Information**
>
> **Yellow Pages** look under 'Introduction Services — Social'.
>
> **Local papers, daily newspapers and women's magazines** often feature ads and special offers in the classified pages.

Speed Dating

This is a new concept designed for the very busy person. It's sort of like one of those job fairs where you bring your résumé along and chat to loads of prospective employers. The fee is between $40 and $60 and places are usually limited so you need to book ahead. On the night in question, participants spend a set period (between 5 and 15 minutes) with each single man. When the bell rings you move along and start talking to someone else. Some speed dating services provide finger food, refreshments and time to mingle. But, even if they don't, you'll have had a chance to talk to all the guys in the room by the end of the session. That's when you fill out a card with the names of the men you'd like to see again, and they do the same. The agency then matches people and provides contacts of anyone interested in you.

The trouble with this approach is it exists on the premise that you can judge a person in a few minutes. That goes against a lot of the advice provided here, but it can be bloody good fun. And that's the spirit to have if you're going to enter the speed dating game. Like *The Weakest Link*, speed dating isn't for the sensitive soul. The risk of leaving with no matching is the equivalent to the 'walk of shame'. But if you keep an open mind and tick enough boxes, you'll be in with a good chance of a date.

Further Information

Look in your local paper under 'Social Scene' or 'What's On' for events near you.

Melbourne

SpeedDating (03) 9544 1191 or www.speeddating.com.au

Flashdate (03) 9527 1184 or www.flashdate.cjb.net

A Dozen Dates in an Hour (03) 9537 3839

Sydney

SpeedDating (02) 9475 4276 or www.speeddating.com.au

Quickdate (02) 9833 0086

Australia-wide

SpeedDating events are also organised in other cities. For more information email info@speeddating.com.au

Telephone Introduction Lines

Anyone with a credit card machine and a phone line can set up a telephone chat line. This means it's a difficult industry to regulate. Before you give this a go, get a timer and keep it by the phone: some 'intro lines' charge more than $5.00 a minute, so your phone bill can creep up if you don't keep your eye on the clock. It might be a good idea to stick to 1900 numbers, which are regulated by Telstra and must adhere to a code of practice. Sometimes, if a line is low on women callers, they'll run a special. So look out for 'ladies free' ads which mean you'll only pay the cost of a connection.

Meeting genuine partners over the phone is questionable, to say the least. Most chat lines are used for flirting or picking up someone for sex or dirty talk, rather than a long-term relationship. *Cosmopolitan*'s Tracey Cox says it's more like 'dial an orgasm than dial a date'.[5] Perhaps it's the modern version of writing 'ring-a-root' on a toilet wall — if you're looking for sex, you'll have plenty of offers.

Further Information

Check the classified pages of women's magazines like *Cleo* and *Cosmopolitan*.

Telecafe 1900 920 500 (calls charged at $1.05 per minute)
Telephone Chat 1900 930 196 (calls charged at $1.05 per minute)
Casual Contacts 1900 910 580 (calls charged at $2.15 per minute)

Paying For Sex

It can be a big mistake to confuse lust and love during your search for lurve. If you've figured out that you're after some physical lurve and you can keep your emotions out of it, paying for sex may be a better option than sleeping with someone you know just because your hormones are on the rampage.

If you decide to pay for sex, phone a legitimate 'escort' service. They supply men (as well as women) who are willing to provide more relief than the usual massage, and it reduces the risk of stranger danger. But, whatever you do, always ensure he wears a condom.

You won't find a male brothel on every corner, but you may find a legitimate masseur willing to go a little bit further. Look for ads that stipulate 'erotic massage'. (Legislation regulating sexual services varies from state to state. Check with your local Department of Consumer Affairs.) *'Matt, full body rub'* could turn out to be terribly disappointing if he comes armed with a bucket, sponge and a bottle of car polish.

You also can try a web search by keying in 'male escorts'. Some services cater exclusively for gay men, but many provide services to heterosexual women. Rates vary from around $100–150 an hour. You can hire a hunk for dinner and a show. Or, skip dinner and go straight to your own private 'show'.

Further Information

Oz Males www.ozwebs.com/1on1manline/

Global Escorts www.globalescorts.com.au

Search for an Escort www.male-escorts.com/search/australia.html

Nero's Boys in Perth (08) 9472 7333

The Boardroom is a Melbourne brothel that caters for men and women. They charge $200 an hour for one man, and $320 an hour for two! (03) 9699 1711 or www.boardroom.com.au

And So ...

As you can see, there are plenty of different services on offer. Meeting a partner in a contrived setting may not be what you had in mind when you were a dreamy teenager, but some of us wanted to marry one of The Bay City Rollers! (Just as well we grew up and got a grip.) Getting others to do the dating dirty work saves time, knock-backs and — when handled correctly — money. So why not swallow that misplaced pride and give it a go?

11. FINDING .... love online

Dear Aunt Lurvinya,

I've heard that it's easy to meet blokes over the Internet but some stuff worries me. Cyber sex for starters, I'm definitely not interested in getting personal with a joystick. Then there are women who've risked everything to shack up with someone they've never met. I'm just not that type of person. Plus, how do you know you're not talking to an axe murderer?

Miss Ann Shuss

Dear Ann,

Cyber-savvy chicks wouldn't go anywhere near a joystick, so relax. It's not that difficult to connect with other normal people over the Internet.

As far as cyber sex is concerned, it's like regular sex. If blokes think they're in with a chance, they'll try it on. That's a fact, especially when there's no risk you'll tip a jug of beer over his head! Just like in real life, if a sleazebag approaches either ignore him, walk away, give him a piece of your mind, or alert the authorities.

With a name like 'Lurvinya' I'm always getting online offers. One hint of lurve and you can guarantee an audience with an entire worldwide web of porn users. It gives me great pleasure to ignore comments like, 'I'd-lurve-to-be-in–ya,' and equal pleasure to get involved in online discussions with members of both sexes. Quite often men open up in ways they just wouldn't when they're in the company of my cleavage. I've spent many hours mulling over the meaning of life, love and minimiser bras with blokes who definitely have more than half a brain. Then again, some nights I seem to cop the idiots who think typing 'ha, ha' after a joke makes it funny.

It's easy to steer clear of sticky situations. Once you start asking intelligent questions, the losers lose interest. So throw caution to the wind, get yourself an anonymous email address, a decent nickname and GO FOR IT.

Aunt Lurvinya

Wired for Lurve

Internet dating is becoming a popular way to meet members of the opposite sex. It's cheap, fast and practical, even on a bad hair day. There's nothing better than a good old-fashioned flirt without having to get up off your bum and stick on false eyelashes! Sure, negotiating line after line of bullshit can be a little daunting; giving people anonymity is like giving them a ticket to deceive. But people who lie or post fake photos usually do so because they have poor self-esteem — or they're idiots!

You also may be tempted to create a new persona, just for a bit of fun. However, if you're serious about finding Lurve, then take a tip from the online experts at People 2 People (http://people.com) who advise:

> If your ultimate goal is to physically meet and establish a relationship with a special, compatible person ... (you have) two options: you can lie your head off and establish an awkward, dishonest relationship or you can lay your heart on the line and let people see you for who you are. The first might be easier, but the second is infinitely more heroic. If you fail at love, it's not from being unattractive or unlucky, but rather, from being uncourageous.[1]

FINDING MEN

The best part about online dating, is that conversations often become surprisingly open, honest and intimate when little things like physical appearances and occupations don't get in the way. For example, men often reveal things to a stranger that they wouldn't dare discuss in person. Not just their sexual fantasies, but the way they *feel* about everything. However, if you find yourself falling for Mr Online, Hollonds' advice is to remember that online communication only occurs on one level:

> We normally form judgements about people on multiple levels, from verbal and non-verbal cues, from the way someone treats you in real life and the way people interact with other people. The Internet only provides you with one level: the written word.

If you manage to sustain regular satisfying online conversations with someone, you may decide to move your friendship to another level. Begin with the phone. If you're still keen after chatting for a while set up a real life rendezvous. You may be nervous. If so, it's because this man is still a stranger.

Cyberlove

In the movie, *You've Got Mail*, Meg Ryan thought she'd met the man of her dreams. When online, Tom Hanks' character was tender, vulnerable and supportive. In real life, he was the ruthless, despicable millionaire who closed down her bookstore! Of course, Meg and Tom eventually got it together. But, remember: you don't live in Hollywood, and the intelligent, age-appropriate Sydney-sider you discover may turn out to be an elderly married transsexual who wears sandals with white socks.

Of course, he could also be Russell Crowe using an assumed name to find a nice, down-to-earth girl. The only way you'll find out is through trial and error. You'll need the same attitude and stamina required for any other lurve-seeking venture — a sense of adventure, a smile (on the inside, too) and the ability to take everything with a grain of salt!

Mistaking Mr Nice Guy for your average axe-murderer isn't the only danger. Virtual flirting is highly addictive and could have you glued to your screen night after night. Don't make cyber love a substitute for the real thing — use it as a tool. You still need to get out in the real world to experience Lurve. If it happens to be with someone you've met over the Internet, I guess you could say you both 'clicked'!

The Basics

You'll need to have access to a computer with a built-in or external modem. Contact a local Internet Service Provider (ISP) to be connected. They may send you some software to install, or take you through a phone tutorial where clicking on a few screen prompts will get you connected. Costs vary, but you should be able to get online for around $25 a month.

Now, simply choose one or more of the sites suggested in this chapter and follow the on screen prompts. If you have difficulty getting into chat rooms, you may need to update your browser. To do this, phone your server and they will guide you through the process.

To ensure anonymity, get a web-based email address. This

means you can keep your personal address for professional purposes or family and friends. When applying for a web-based email address, some forms have a box for your real name that may appear on emails you send. For online dating, it's a good idea to supply a false name to protect your identity. Before you get going, visit: www.alphalink.com.au, for information about downloads and tips for protecting yourself against a virus. Or, do a search using 'virus protection' to find other support services. If you do experience problems, ring your ISP for technical advice.

The next step, and perhaps the key to your success, is choosing a nickname. In chat rooms, people often use nicknames as a basis for deciding whether they'll make contact. For example, think about the type of bloke that you want to attract before choosing a name like 'RogerMeSenseless'! Consider the impression you want to make and choose a name that reflects those qualities. Of course, you can use your own name and change your nickname to suit your mood.

Get onto IT

There are several ways to use the Internet as an avenue for finding love. There are online introduction agencies (see below), chat rooms and online interest groups. However you decide to plan your search, keep an open mind. You may not meet a man straight off, but you may make new friendships with men and women. Perhaps if your social life revolves around dinners with your married friends, you may simply be looking for a like-minded woman who is keen to team up for nights out on the town.

ONLINE DATING SERVICES

Online matchmaking is big business. Most services are free to join — you simply fill out a profile form, which is then posted on a database that can be accessed by other members. That includes you, so if you like what you've read about someone else, you can contact them.

FINDING ... love online

That's where the cost comes in: most services use a 'stamp' system that involves buying a book of stamps and using one each time you send a message. Some require that you sign up for a specific period, which gives you full access during that time. If you don't want to pay, wait for other members to send you a message. Sometimes you can send a 'virtual kiss' which lets the other person know you're interested in talking. If they want to talk back, they will have to pay.

TRUE TALES...
The first day I joined a partner matching service, I received a message from John. I was itching to read what he had to say, but when I tried I was sent to the 'subscribe' page and had to sign up for a minimum of 5 days at $9.95. The next day I received an email telling me that ten men who lived in my region were waiting to talk to me and that I was top of the desirable list for four of them. They were all supposedly tall and handsome. It was a big ego boost.
Carol, 35

Some services will email you whenever someone who suits your criteria joins up. This is the most secure method because your email address remains private until you choose to give it out. But you still have to pay to make the initial contact.

TRUE TALES...
I've 'met' four men through an online partner matching service. I corresponded by email with one guy for a long time, and I was ready to meet him. Then I asked why his kids lived with him instead of their mother and I found out that he lived with her too. Apparently, he wanted to check out the 'talent' before he left her.

I dated the second guy a couple of times but we just didn't click. Another was nice via email, but when I agreed to meet, he got really demanding about weekends away, so I said, 'No way'.

The next guy I met was really nice, and I fell for him big time. I guess it's just like meeting guys any other way — you've got to try the drongos to find the dreamboats. Except, because you don't get to see what they look like straightaway, it may take a bit longer.
Simone, 30

Apparently, posting a photo offers a better chance of receiving messages. Once you've made contact through the agency it's up to you to continue communicating through conventional email or to meet up in a chat channel.

Further Information

There are plenty of online partner matching services to choose from. Here are a few starters:

Catch.com lets you peruse profiles for no charge and provides plenty of 'I found my perfect man' testimonials for inspiration; www.catch.com.au

RSVP.com claims to be Australia's largest dating site and is user-friendly; www.RSVP.com.au

Friend Finder can help you find pen pals and activity partners as well as soul mates; www.friendfinder.com

Soul Mates posts profiles including photos. Each profile has a personal introduction, so you do get a little bit more of an idea of what they are like. You can also search in your region and for single Christians; www.soulmates.com.au

Udate claims to assure privacy and will send you emails from people who've sent you a message, or indicate that you're on their desirable list. It's an international site, but you can do a regional search to find people on your side of the planet; www.udate.com

CHAT ROOMS

You can log on to any chat channel at any time to find thousands of people waiting to talk to you! It can be a little daunting and confusing at first, especially because it's often hard to follow a conversation. This is because people in chat rooms speak a different language; a shorthand slang that can take a bit of getting used to.

It's called 'messaging' and it consists of sets of abbreviations that seem like fragments of conversations. The main chat window that appears on your screen is usually only a jumping

FINDING ... love online

board into 'one-on-one' conversations. Once you hook up with another user, all public conversation stops. It takes some practice, but once you know the lingo, things become much easier.

Learning Chat-Room Lingo

If you don't understand what someone has written, ask.

Using capital letters is the equivalent of shouting, so it can be considered RUDE!

People often substitute faces ☺ for words. To draw a smiley face, just type a colon, then a right hand bracket. Some computers will convert it to a face. A sad face ☹ is made with a colon and a left-hand bracket.

Some abbreviations:

    a/s/l — age, sex and location

    lol — laughing out loud

    rofl — roll on floor laughing

    brb — be right back

    btw — by the way

    b4n — bye for now

    bg — big grin

    f2f — face to face

    ayt — are you there?

Prime Consulting lists over 400 acronyms and 47 smileys; www.pconsulting.com.au/netspeak

To speak to someone one-on-one (called a 'whisper' or 'going private') double click on their name. In some sites you right click instead. A small window will open up on your screen (and theirs) where you can key in a personal message. It might be as simple as 'hi'. In some rooms, this appears at the bottom of the screen as a little speech 'balloon'.

Keep an eye on the bottom of your screen for whispers sent by others. Even if you don't say anything, when you join a room, your arrival is announced, and sometimes your name will be enough to motivate other people to make contact. If you don't get any hits, you may have to get involved in the conversation going on in the main chat window. Just jump in and see what happens. You've got nothing to lose.

TRUE TALES...

> Talking on the Internet is fantastic because you can go up to anyone and say 'hi'. In fact, you are actually more likely to be able to initiate a conversation in a chat room than in real life. The most common introductory question is A/S/L? This means age/sex/location. This really annoys me as I only ever go in to have a gossip. But I suppose if you're looking to meet someone it's useful to know their age, gender and city.
>
> Julie, 30

If someone is trying to make contact with you, a dialogue box or the whisper icon will appear on your screen. You can choose to answer it or to ignore it, depending on the content. The main chat window will remain open, so you can keep an eye on what's going on there. When you get better at chatting, you'll be able to keep more than one conversation going at a time — which can sometimes be very confusing!

Be safe, not sorry

Protect your identity and home address until you feel certain you want to share it with a stranger.

Use a web-based email account available through Hotmail or Yahoo or visit www.emailaddresses.com for a comprehensive listing of free services on offer.

When meeting Internet friends for the first time, always meet in public and tell a friend to phone your mobile after half an hour to see if everything's okay.

If you find yourself in an uncomfortable or compromising situation that is threatening or illegal, contact your local police.

FINDING ... love online

There are loads of chat rooms to try. General chat rooms tend to attract teenagers and young adults, so choose rooms with a particular focus like romance, books, or topical issues. Lifestyle groupings (age and family situation) are also a good bet. Then, of course, there are 'adult' rooms — enough said about those.

Some Places to chat

Ninemsn *has lots of chat rooms to choose from. Blush is specifically for romance, or check out some of the peer groups where you'll have a better chance of chatting with someone local; chat.ninemsn.com.au/default.msnw*

ICQ *has a range of chat rooms that allow you to type in 'ignore (name)' to block anyone you don't like the sound of. 'Just Friends' and 'Looking For Love' under 'romance' are friendly international rooms; web.icq.com*

Yahoo *has regular chat rooms and others with a particular focus. In busy rooms, it's best to click on the names of other chatters and go straight for the one-on-one chats rather than jump into the main room. Or, wait for someone to contact you. A window will open on your screen when someone makes contact. Because this is an international site, it may be more difficult to link up with people close to home; www.chat.yahoo.com*

AOL *has local and international chat rooms. You can access the international chats once you have registered. But to access the Australian rooms you need to sign up and make AOL your server; www.aol.com.au*

INTEREST GROUPS

Online communication doesn't just mean mindless chitchat or steamy gossip about celebrities. Once you know your way around, you can get involved in all sort of interesting online conversations and activities. Going into a chat room for a specific purpose or discussing important issues through bulletin boards, discussion groups and forums can help you hook up with other like-minded people.

TRUE TALES....

Last year, I met a guy in a trivia chat room. We talked for half an hour before exchanging email addresses. Soon we were emailing every day. He lived in Singapore, so we started talking on the telephone. Eventually, our conversations became very intimate and we were dying to meet. He was coming to Sydney on business so we decided to meet up.

I was still a bit paranoid, so I took a friend to the pub where we planned to meet. But when we locked eyes, she had to leave because the sparks were flying! Four wonderful days followed. When we said goodbye at the airport, he said it felt like he was losing his right arm. But it ended in tears when he was transferred to Canada. I think he'd already met someone, but it took me a long time to get over it.

Charlotte, 34

If you like playing games — not the emotional kind — online gaming rooms are a great place to try your hand at chess or trivia. If you have a particular passion, simply surf the web for relevant sites. You'll no doubt find one with a scheduled chat time or bulletin boards where you can post messages on particular topics or answer other people's queries. Then, it's a matter of exchanging email addresses so you can chat on a regular basis.

TRUE TALES....

I played on Yahoo's Chess website a couple of times. I was a shocker of a player, so everyone loved playing me to get more points! I collected the email addresses of people from all over the world: Canada, USA, France and even a guy from St Kilda!

Months later, I found the list of email addresses while cleaning my room. Instead of tossing it out, I decided to send some messages. Believe it, or not, everyone replied.

Eventually, I became friends with the guy in St Kilda. We emailed every day for two weeks. When our emails became longer I suggested we started talking on the phone to save time (and so I could hear his voice). We talked every day and I never got bored. He had such a great personality I didn't care what he looked like.

We finally met up, and had a fun night; we carried on just like we did over the phone. I got to know him more than I would have if

FINDING ... love online

I'd met him in a pub. It was nice to know that a guy liked me for my personality without looks getting in the way. I'm not sure if I'll see him again, but we're still in regular contact.

Geeta, 28

Further Information

Do a general web search using words relating to your interests. Some of your 'hits' might include sites with chats or discussion groups.

Yahoo Games games.yahoo.com

ICQ Game Partners click on 'Game Partners' in the list on the right of the page; www.icq.com

Sports chats and forums www.sportnet.com.au/Portal/Chat.Forum.cfm

Political activist discussion groups such as www.greenleft.org.au/others.htm#NEWSGROUPS.

Message boards on a range of topics www.web.icq.com

CONCLUSION

A Final Word from Aunt Lurvinya

Dear Lurvies,

I never said that finding lurve in the modern world was gonna be easy. Life, as we know it, is complicated, and that includes how we relate to men. In their own merry way, blokes are just as confused as we are. But when under stress, instead of agonising over the issues, they just do something else. I often come across men eager to dispel the myth that they can only do one thing at a time: one walked to the fridge with his baby on his hip and shouted, 'Look! I'm doing two things at a time.' He then extracted a beer and held it up to prove his point. I wasn't impressed. We all know beer is the exception.

Ask yourself how you would feel if you were one of the less evolved of the species. After all, when men measure themselves against women they soon realise that we have something over them — like being able to grow another human being inside our body and nourish it until it is old enough to feed itself. Sure, we need their help for this. But they know that once they've planted the seed, we can do very well on our own. That's what scares them. And, that, my dears, was how patriarchy was born. And we're still fighting our way out of that tunnel.

Change takes time and women are now moving from wanting equality to wanting our 'differences' recognised. We want the freedom to become who we are, and men want the same thing. My guess is, it's hard for the average bloke to understand what we want.

Time to give the poor bastards a break and get angry about the things that really matter. Like the silly games men play when all we want to find out is whether they want to see us again.

Like phoning when they say they will. Most of us are available 24/7 via mobiles, email, message bank and SMS text messaging. The more technology we have at our fingertips the less excuses a bloke has. So it's no wonder we become obsessed. Most of us cope better than Bridget Jones (who repeatedly checked to see if Daniel or Mark had phoned while she was out), but only marginally.

How refreshing to meet a man who phones when he says he will. No waiting games, no bullshit. And how liberating it would be if we felt that we could also pick up the phone and talk to him without the fear that we'll scare him off or break an old-fashioned 'dating rule'. If we're sick of games then why don't we just throw the rulebook out the window and go with our gut feelings? If he runs a mile, then he'd have run regardless.

Not quite ready to give up all the 'how to snare your man' stuff you've heard? If you find this kind of advice useful, you're probably already a player: flirting comes naturally, and you use magazines and books to develop your technique. If you're just not that type of woman, then why bash your head against a brick wall? You're going to have to find a way to enter the dating maze by simply being yourself. Use your intuition to judge how a date is going.

What you wear, how you sit, or if you choose to sleep with him on a first date (blah, blah, blah) really has little to do with eventual compatibility. It's just a matter of respecting yourself and

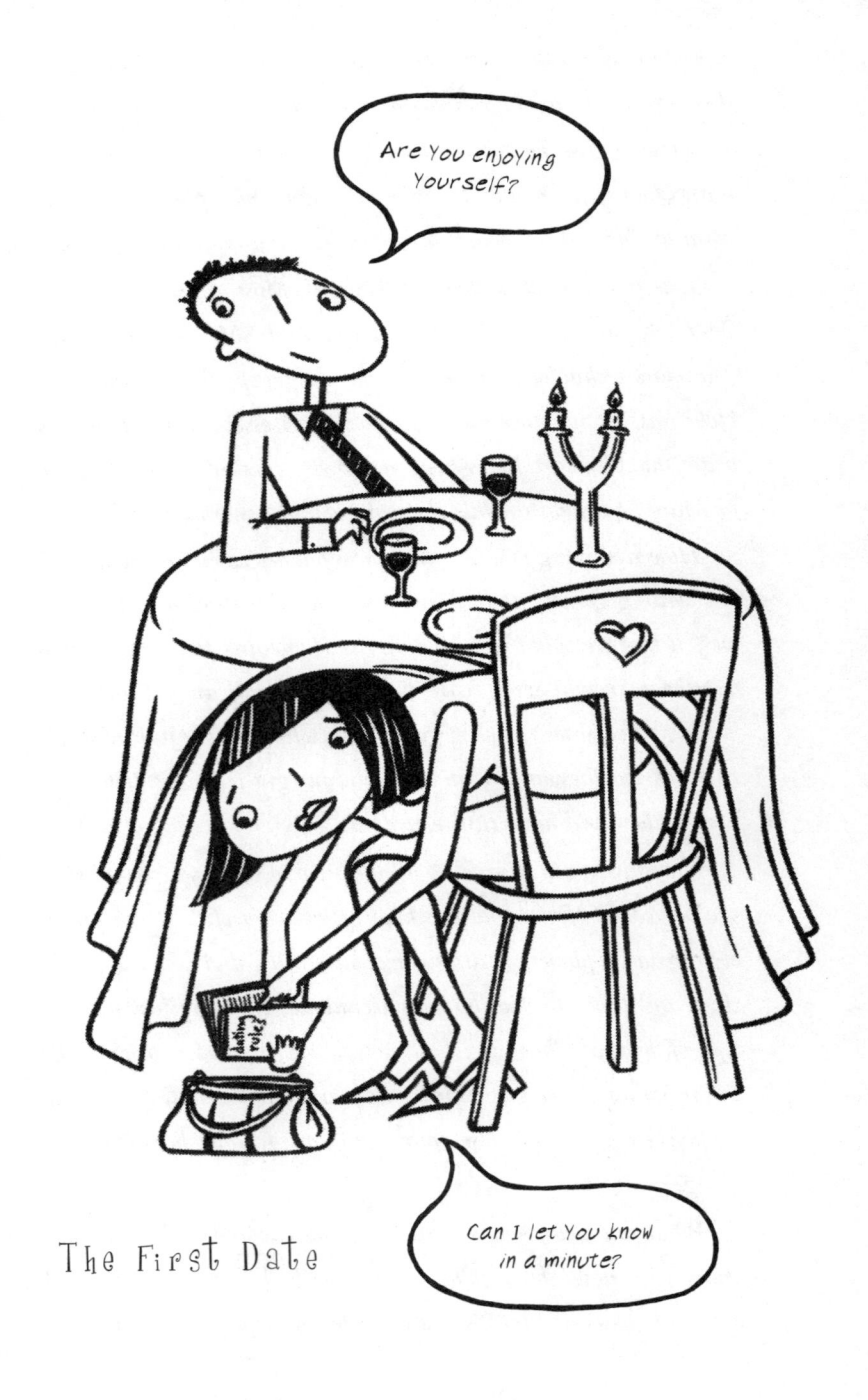

The First Date

others, and celebrating the fact that every person you meet, and possibly date, is different. And that's what leads to love.

Always remember to keep a level head: romantic love can send you spinning off your axis, which can be great. Just avoid the temptation to project your fantasies onto someone before you know what they're really like. It's also best to take each day one step at a time. Instead of planning for the future, why not concentrate on enjoying the present?

Whatever you do, don't try to turn Mr Wrong into Mr Right. It will never happen and there's nothing wrong with being on your own. Not everyone in a relationship is happy, and love isn't the only ingredient for happiness. So, think about what you really want out of life and get to work.

If you still haven't found lurve then ask yourself the following ...

- Do you really want to find love, or are you actually happy on your own?
- Are you hanging onto baggage that is sabotaging your relationships?
- Do you harbour narcissistic traits that have turned you into your own worst enemy?
- Have you thought of moving to China, where an estimated 90 million men are looking for a partner?

Good luck and let me know how you go.

Aunt Lurvinya
auntlurvinya@hotmail.com

Notes

Part One Finding Love

1 FINDING ... it hard

1. David M. Buss, *The Evolution of Desire*, Basic Books, New York, 1994, p. 49.

2 FINDING ... the meaning of love

1. Simon Andreae, *Anatomy of Desire*, Little, Brown and Company, London, 1998, p. 182.
2. Dorothy Tennov, *Love and Limerence: The Experience of Being in Love*, Scarborough House, New York, 1999
3. Danny Lee, Danny Lee's Book Reviews website at: www.dannyreviews.com/h/Love_Limerence.html.
4. Interview, Helen Harman and Julie Fitness, 2001.
5. Simon Andreae, op.cit., pp. 204–6.
6. Paul Fenton-Smith, *Finding Your Soul Mate*, Simon and Schuster, Sydney, 2001, p. 3.
7. Robert A. Johnson, *The Psychology of Romantic Love*, Arkana, London, 1987, p. (ix).
8. Simon Andreae, op. cit., p. 205.
9. John Gottman and Nan Silver, *The Seven Principles For Making Marriage Work*, Orion, London, 1999, p. 19.
10. Simon Andreae, op. cit., p. 217.
11. Erica Jong, *What Do Women Want?*, Harper Collins, New York, 1998, p. 134.

3 FINDING ... the perfect man

1. Dr Janet Hall, *Sex Wise*, Random House, Sydney, 2000, p. 23.
2. John Gray, *Men Are From Mars, Women Are From Venus*, Harper Collins, London, 1992, pp. 59-60.
3. Dr Toby Green, *If You Really Loved Me*, Random House, Sydney, 1996, p. 48.
4. Ibid, pp. 47–8.
5. Interview, Helen Harman and Fiona Papps, 2001.

6 Anthony Giddens, *The Transformation of Intimacy*, Polity Press, London, 1992, p. 58.
7 Bradley Trevor Greive, *Looking For Mr Right*, Random House, Sydney, 2001, p. 41.
8 Cyndi Kaplan-Freiman, *Sexy, Sane and Solvent*, HarperCollins, Sydney, 2000, p. 67.
9 Simon Andreae, op. cit., p. 48.
10 Dr Rosie King, 'Relationships', *Woman's Day* (Australia), 13/12/99.
11 David M. Buss, op. cit., pp. 38–41.
12 John Gray, *What Your Mother Couldn't Tell You & Your Father Didn't Know*, HarperCollins, New York, 1994, p. 23.
13 Erica Jong, op. cit., p. 129.

Part Two Finding Self

4 FINDING ... body confidence

1 Naomi Wolf, *The Beauty Myth*, Vintage, London, 1990, p. 10.
2 Germaine Greer, *The Whole Woman*, Doubleday, London, 1999, p. 32.
3 Simon Andreae, op. cit., p. 55.
4 Cyndi Tebbel, *The Body Snatchers: How The Media Shapes Women*, Finch Publishing, Sydney, 2000, pp. 51–2.
5 Interview, Helen Harman and Cyndi Tebbel, 2001.
6 Cyndi Tebbel, op. cit., p. (xi).
7 David M. Buss, op. cit., p. 53.
8 Simon Andreae, op. cit., pp. 169–170.
9 Ibid, pp. 209–210.
10 'What Women Want', a *Marie Claire* forum, Channel 10 (Australia), 15/10/01.
11 Cyndi Kaplan-Freiman, op. cit., p. 24.
12 Ross Smith, *The Principles of Metabolic Fitness*, Lothian Books, Melbourne, 2001, p. 40.
13 Cyndi Kaplan-Freiman, op. cit., p. 24.
14 Naomi Wolf, op. cit., p. 274.
15 Ibid, p. 290.
16 Cyndi Tebbel, op. cit., p. 87.

17   Ibid, p. (xiii).
18   Germaine Greer, op. cit., p. 3.

5 FINDING ... love with attitude

1   Jennifer Garth, 'Six Myths You Need to Leave Behind', *Body & Soul* magazine, *The Herald Sun* (Melbourne), 30/9/01.
2   Judith Sills, *Loving Men More, Needing Men Less*, Penguin Books, New York, 1996, p. 17.
3   Nita Tucker, *How Not To Stay Single*, Vermillion, London, 1996, p. 24.
4   Ibid, p. 85.
5   Stephanie Dowrick, 'What Happiness Is', *Good Weekend* magazine, *The Age* (Melbourne), 29/9/01.
6   Toby Green, op. cit., p. 235.
7   Ibid, p. 32.
8   Nita Tucker, op. cit., p. 83.
9   Interview, Helen Harman and Cyndi Tebbel, 2001.
10 Interview, Helen Harman and Fiona Papps, 2001.
11 Tracey Cox, *Hot Relationships: How To Have One*, Bantam Books, Sydney, 1999, p. 5.
12 Jordan Kelly, *The Great Aussie Soulmate Search*, Wrightbooks, Melbourne, 1998, p. 8.
13 Judith Sills, op. cit., p. 15.
14 Nita Tucker, op. cit., p. 117.
15 Ayala Malach Pines, *Falling In Love: Why We Choose The Lovers We Choose*, Routledge, New York, 1999, p. 46.
16 Nita Tucker, op. cit., pp. 47–8.

6 FINDING ... love with baggage

1   Judith Sills, op. cit., p. 36.
2   Judith Sills, *Excess Baggage*, Penguin Books, New York, 1993, pp. 10–11.
3   'Prayer for September 26, 2000', from www.aboutyourbreakup.com.
4   Richard G. Whiteside and Francis E. Steinberg, *When Your Lover Leaves You*, Pan Macmillan, New York, 2000.

5   Interview, Helen Harman and Julie Fitness, 2001.
6   Toby Green, op. cit., p. 222.
7   Interview, Helen Harman and Anne Hollonds, 2001.
8   Cyndi Kaplan, Lifesavers, *A Woman's Guide to Survival and Self-Esteem*, Lansdowne Publishing, Sydney, 1993, p. 177.
9   Interview, Helen Harman and Julie Fitness, 2001
10 Nita Tucker, op. cit., p. 38.
11 Cyndi Kaplan-Freiman, op. cit., p. 67.
12 Interview, Helen Harman and Anne Hollonds, 2001.
13 Tracey Cox, op. cit., p. 6.
14 Linda Georgian, *How To Attract your Ideal Mate*, A Fireside Book, New York, 1999, p. 115.
15 Sills, *Loving Men More, Needing Men Less*, p. 11.
16 Laura Doyle, *The Surrendered Wife: a practical guide for finding intimacy, passion, and peace with a man*, Simon & Schuster, New York, 2001.
17 Ibid, p. 24.
18 Stephanie Dowrick, op. cit.
19 Judith Sills, op. cit., pp. 18–19.
20 Dr Bruce A. Stevens, 'Mirror, Mirror', *Canberra Clinical & Forensic Psychology*, Australia, 2000, p. 7.
21 Ibid, pp. 8–9.
22 Sills, *Excess Baggage*, pp. 101–2.
23 Sills, *Loving Men More, Needing Men Less*, p. 39.
24 Linda Georgian, op. cit., p. 50.
25 Ibid, p. 51.
26 Simon Andreae, op. cit., p. 182.
27 John Gray, *Mars and Venus on a Date*, Hodder Headline, Sydney, 1997, p. 17.
28 Riane Eisler, *Sacred Pleasure*, Doubleday, Sydney, 1996, p. 15.
29 Germaine Greer, op. cit., p. 181.

7 FINDING ... love with kids in tow

1   Dr Judy Kuriansky, *The Complete Idiot's Guide to Dating*, Alpha Books, New York, 1999, p. 350.
2   Ibid, p. 352.
3   Ibid, p. 351.

4   Ibid, p. 349.
5   Dr Toby Green, op. cit., pp. 166–7.

Part Three   Finding Men

8   FINDING ... love in your own backyard

1   Nita Tucker, op. cit., p. 18.
2   Tracey Cox, op. cit., p. 70.
3   Ibid, p. 69.

10   FINDING ... love with paid help

1   Jordan Kelly, op. cit., pp. 2–6.
2   Sills, *Loving Men More, Needing Men Less*, p. 11.
3   Ayala Malach Pines, op. cit., p. 66.
4   Cameron Stewart, 'Make Love and War', *The Weekend Australian*, 10–11/11/01.
5   Tracey Cox, op. cit., p. 80.

11   FINDING ... love online

1   *Smooch* e-zine, at www.people2people.com/zine.